THE PETER PYRAMID
WHY GOVERNMENTS AND INSTITUTIONS RISE TO THEIR LEVELS OF INCOMPETENCE

Poor Bronsky, he's a little more than halfway finished with building his pyramid. But I don't think he'll ever finish it all the way to the top. You see, the more successful he is, the bigger he wants to build the bottom of the pyramid. And the bigger he builds the bottom, the farther it is to the top. Frankly, if he ever felt he could reach the top of it he'd never start building it in the first place.—MEL BROOKS

THE PETER PYRAMID
IN ACTION

Today a public school education costs over $25,000 per pupil, yet SAT scores are dropping. Why? Because high-level bureaucracy always produces low-level output. The following was sent by a high school principal to parents inviting them to a meeting about a new educational program. The invitation included a description of the program which said, in part:

Our school's Cross-Graded, Multi-Ethnic, Individualized Learning Program is designed to enhance the concept of an Open-Ended Learning Program with emphasis on a continuum of multi-ethnic academically enriched learning, using the identified intellectually gifted child as the agent or director of his own learning. Major emphasis is on cross-graded, multi-ethnic learning with the main objective being to learn respect for the uniqueness of a person.

MORE. . . .

THE PETER PYRAMID: SYSTEMS START SMALL AND GROW TO OCCUPY ALL OUR TIME AND SPACE.

Once out of school, our young people are faced with many important decisions, such as voting into office bureaucrats who use phrases like these:

"public information strategies on the government's overall response"—*official lies*

"a favorable success ratio"—*winning*

"low-density seating"—*first class airfare*

"influence of the pricing environment"—*cost*

"improving the interface"—*making friends*

PETER'S BUREAUCRATIC PRINCIPLES

1. The bureaucracy must be protected.
2. Bureaucratic survival is contingent on an increased budget.
3. Bureaucracies breed.
4. Bureaucracies avoid doing anything for the first time.
5. Large bureaucracies grow from small ones, but do not perform the functions for which they were initially established.
6. Bureaucracies attract a type of personality adapted to thrive in them.
7. Bureaucracies value internal harmony over output or service.
8. Bureaucracies defend the status quo long after the quo has lost its status.
9. An individual with real leadership ability wanting to become a bureaucrat is as likely as a competent jockey wanting to become a horse.
10. In an emergency a bureaucracy will offer you every assistance short of help.

"The pyramids are solidly built, have a nice view from the top, and serve as a resting place for the dead."
——GERALD A. MICHAELSON

Bantam Books by Dr. Laurence J. Peter
Ask your bookseller for the books you have missed

THE PETER PRINCIPLE (with Raymond Hull)
THE PETER PYRAMID
PETER'S QUOTATIONS
WHY THINGS GO WRONG

The
Peter
Pyramid

—— *OR* ——

Will We Ever Get the Point?

Dr. Laurence J. Peter

ILLUSTRATED BY MATT WUERKER

BANTAM BOOKS
TORONTO · NEW YORK · LONDON · SYDNEY · AUCKLAND

THE PETER PYRAMID

*A Bantam Book / published by arrangement with
William Morrow & Company*

PRINTING HISTORY

William Morrow & Company edition published January 1986

Bantam edition / January 1987

*Bantam Books are published by Bantam Books, Inc. Its trademark, consisting of
the words "Bantam Books" and the portrayal of a rooster, is Registered in U.S.
Patent and Trademark Office and in other countries. Marca Registrada. Bantam
Books, Inc., 666 Fifth Avenue, New York, New York 10103.*

To Sid Taylor, in appreciation
of his concept of
System Simplification

Contents

The
Peter
Pyramid

1

Pyramid Power

The future ain't what it used to be. —ARTHUR C. CLARKE

We live in a wonderful world beautifully suited to our needs. We are not required to approve of all the things or all the individuals in it in order to believe that generally the world is a friendly place that gives us sustenance while challenging us to sharpen our wits, stimulate our creativity, and test our courage.

> Innumerable confusions and a feeling of despair invariably emerge in periods of great technological and cultural transition. —MARSHALL McLUHAN

Today the world is full of problems, but I do not believe that the human race, endowed with the capacity to explore and understand, was intended to commit suicide. I do not interpret our crisis as the death struggle of civilization. It could just as well be the birth struggle of a new civilization emerging and the beginnings of a brighter future.

> When written in Chinese, the word crisis is composed of two characters—one represents danger and the other represents opportunity. —JOHN F. KENNEDY

Interest in the future is growing rapidly because the future is happening so fast. In less than fifty years the global population has nearly doubled and we have entered the atomic age, the space age, the computer age, and the age of robotics. Few agree as to where all this is leading, but it is clear that a tidal wave of change is sweeping through the world.

Some of today's problems we have never experienced before, and we have come to realize, finally, the inter-relatedness of all things. Every action we take is projected forward in time and outward in space, and every attempt at solving a problem seems to create new problems.

Why do hungry nations export food while the richest suffer demoralizing recessions? Why is it that revolutions against tyrannical regimes become tyrannies themselves? And why, with so much American creativity, is our industrial productivity declining?

In other words, how does it happen that things turn out so differently from what common sense would expect?

> It is the familiar that usually eludes us in life. What is before our nose is what we see last.
> —WILLIAM BARRETT

One way to find answers to these questions is to seek a deeper understanding of the pyramidal structure of human organizations. For in these structures we see the microcosm of the things that puzzle us about the world.

> Man cannot live without seeking to describe and explain the universe.   —SIR ISAIAH BERLIN

When our study of human organizations is successful, it leads us to concepts that make our lives and our world more intelligible to us. When things are intelligible we have more of a sense of participation, and when they are unintelligible we have a sense of estrangement. So, when the world appears to be a chaotic mass of unrelated elements, we are in need of a new formulation to give meaning to those events.

> We do not know where or how to start our analysis of this world. There is no wisdom to tell us. Even the scientific tradition does not tell us. It only tells us where and how other people started, and where they got to. —SIR KARL POPPER

In an earlier work, *The Peter Principle,* I showed how an individual within a hierarchy tends to rise to his or her level of incompetence. I called this concept a principle, not a law, because it was neither universal, immutable, nor inevitable. It only described a tendency of an individual to climb or be promoted from one level of competence to the next until arrival at a level of incapacity. Unfortunately, this is where he or she usually remains, frustrating co-workers, eroding the efficiency of the organization, or at the highest level, leading the country into one disaster after another. The principle did not exclude the happy possibility that a good teacher would refuse promotion into administration, that a successful salesperson would decline to become sales manager, that a competent mayor would not seek to become governor or president. And there are also those who remain outside established hierarchies and who regularly experience the joys of individual accomplishment so seldom felt by those in the rat race.

> One man's ceiling is another man's floor. —DAVID LEVINE

The Peter Principle's contribution was threefold. First, it provided an explanation for why so many things go wrong and why so many individuals are incompetent. Second, it warned that unbridled ambition and mindless escalation could lead to disappointment while at the same time it provided management with motivation to re-examine its promotion policies. Third, and probably of greater importance, it gave us a satirical view of ourselves, the human condition, and our ways of managing our affairs.

> Laugh at yourself first, before anyone else can.
> —ELSA MAXWELL

What the Peter Principle did for the individual, the Peter Pyramid will do for the system. The Peter Pyramid shows how whole systems can escalate to their levels of incompetence and how this can be avoided.

> Life is rather like a tin of sardines, we're all of us looking for the key. —ALAN BENNETT

In order to grasp the full significance of the Peter Pyramid, we must first take a brief look at the traditional or base-down pyramid and the myths and realities of pyramid power as it has influenced human behavior through the ages. This is essential for two reasons: (1) Frequently when we think we are building a base-down pyramid we are doing just the opposite; and (2) a Peter Pyramid can grow within an apparently stable organizational structure and render it useless.

> We are going to have to be rather clever people if we are going to escape from our own cleverness in the past. —SIR MARK OLIPHANT

Soldiers, from the summit of yonder pyramids forty centuries look down upon you.
—NAPOLEON BONAPARTE *(addressing his troops in Egypt, July 21, 1798)*

PERFECT PROTOTYPE

Of the Seven Wonders of the ancient world, the Pyramids of Egypt, the Hanging Gardens of Babylon, the Statue of Zeus at Olympia, the Temple of Artemis at Ephesus, the Mausoleum of Halicarnassus, the Colossus of Rhodes, and the Lighthouse or Pharos of Alexandria, the pyramids are the oldest, dating from 2686 to 2160 B.C. They are the only ancient wonders in existence today. This fact in itself should be cause enough to inquire not only how they came into being, but how they are able to remain standing.

Glossary of Terms

EGYPT: *Where the Israelites would still be if Moses had been a bureaucrat.*

PYRAMID: *Proof that there isn't always room at the top.*

PYRAMID EXPERT: *(1) A creatively imaginative individual a long way from Egypt, (2) one who never gets the point.*

The history of the Egyptian pyramids is shrouded in mystery, and many theories exist regarding their meaning. Were they just elaborate tombs? Were they edifices created by long-forgotten architectural or engineering geniuses? Were they public works projects? Were they depositories of

Divine Revelation expressed in geometrical terms? My studies have led me to the following answers.

IMPERISHABLE TOMBS

In ancient Egypt it was believed that the survival of the spirit after death required the preservation and protection of the body. With this in mind, the early pharaohs devoted considerable effort during their lifetime to preparation for death. Early royal tombs were chambers carved inside of mountains, rather than free-standing structures. The tunnels leading to these vaults were sealed and hidden against intruders. Testimony to the success of the mountain crypts is the fact that King Tutankhamen's tomb, built in the fourteenth century B.C., was not discovered until A.D. 1922.

The pharaohs attempted to outdo each other in their funeral preparation, and so the stylized, custom-built mountain or pyramid became popular. As a burial vault it was a complete flop. The pyramid was easy to find and its purpose was no secret, thus making the job of grave robbing much simpler. None of the pyramids held the mummified remains of the monarch who built it, or his store of treasure, for long. The edifice was a great status symbol but a functional disaster. Pyramids remain as monuments to perpetuate the memory of the long forgotten.

> I wouldn't be caught dead in one of those things.
> —ANCIENT EGYPTIAN
> ON VIEWING THE GREAT PYRAMID

ENGINEERING MARVEL

The Egyptians already had government bureaucracy, taxes, hieroglyphics, and metal weapons before they started building pyramids. There is no technological breakthrough that provides an explanation for the sudden popularity of the pyramid. Limestone blocks had long been cut and polished for other purposes. The quarrying of the limestone and hauling it to the building site were accomplished by huge amounts of manpower rather than by any newly discovered technology.

Exaggerated Feats

The Great Pyramid of Giza rose to a height of 481 feet. Its base covered thirteen acres. It consisted of 2,300,000 blocks of limestone, producing a total volume of 3,057,000 cubic yards, not counting the passages and the king's burial chambers. The manpower and the administration required to accomplish such a construction project are certainly impressive and should not be underestimated, but the technology and engineering were much simpler than commonly believed. The largest blocks used in the base weighed up to a maximum of two and a half tons. Although a dozen blocks of this weight could be carried by a modern truck, dragging them over the sand by man-and-mulepower was an arduous task. But they were nothing like the enormous ones depicted in novels and movies. From the heavy base blocks the stones decreased in size as the construction progressed upward. The average block was only about 6¾ cubic feet, so the upper stones were relatively small.

Zoser's Step Pyramid of Saqqara is the oldest structure still standing. Its step design reflects a belief held that the route to heaven was via a stairway. Succeeding pyramids were constructed with flat, sloping sides because later it was believed that the ascent to heaven was along a sun's ray.

Building a pyramid seems a simple task requiring mainly a lot of hard work. Just pile the stones in receding layers, one on top of another, until you have only one stone on top, and you're finished. That is what they thought until they had the first slant-sided structure, the Meidum Pyramid, well under construction. The ruined state of this pyramid indicates that the pressure caused by its own weight was not evenly distributed, causing the limestone to crumble. The Meidum Pyramid was intended to be the most impressive edifice of all time, but was on its way to becoming the most impressive ruin before it was completed.

The next grand-scale pyramid was designed to reach a new height and was one-third finished when the problem at Meidum was detected. The angle of elevation on the new project was lowered, resulting in the strange-looking construction called the Bent Pyramid.

Pyramid architects later returned to the original slope, using an improved internal structure and accurately fitted buttress stones. This is a classic example of trial-and-error method and not of engineering genius. The Egyptian pyramids are a monument to simple persistence and are credited with being the largest things in the world ever built for the wrong reasons.

When Cecil B. DeMille was asked why he had turned out so many films based on the Bible, he answered, "Why let two thousand years of publicity go to waste?"

Experience is a marvelous thing. It enables you to recognize a mistake whenever you make it again.
—FRANKLIN P. JONES

When I asked my friends about the building of the pyramids, they describe scenes of thousands of slaves dragging blocks of stone weighing hundreds of tons while being driven by the whips of slavemasters. It appears that their knowledge was derived from such film epics as The Ten Commandments. *The known facts are at great variance with the movie version.*

"Although some slaves were employed in building the pyramids, most of the workers were peasants . . . employed when the Nile was flooding. Workers were not regarded as expendable; overseers and foremen took pride in reporting on their safety and welfare. In a record of a quarrying expedition to the desert, a leader boasted that he had not lost a man or mule. The labourers were organized into gangs; skilled workers cut granite for the columns, architraves, doorjambs, lintels, and casing blocks. Masons and other craftsmen dressed, polished, and laid the blocks and probably erected ramps to drag the stones into place." (Encyclopaedia Britannica III)

> Who shall doubt the secret hid
> Under Egypt's pyramid!
> Was that the contractor did
> Cheops out of several millions.
> —RUDYARD KIPLING

PUBLIC WORKS PROJECTS

As a public works project to create employment during the annual three-month flood season of the Nile, pyramid construction must have seemed ideal. The only drawback was that although a hundred thousand men could be employed in laying the base, fewer and fewer men were required as the structure grew, until at the top only a handful were required to lay the capstone. A skeleton crew worked year round for twenty years to complete each large pyramid, but the greatest labor was provided by the seasonal workers. To provide full employment, maintain morale, and build patriotic pride, several pyramids were under construction at the same time. Constructing one pyramid at a time would have produced full employment only once every twenty years. This may be why the pyramid-building boom was relatively short-lived. The five largest pyramids were built in less than one century.

Figures Don't Lie

Some of the relationships between the measurements of the Great Pyramid and historical events are impressive. On the other hand, if you took enough measurements of a shoebox in every possible direction and then searched for links between these measurements and the multitudinous events of history, you would eventually identify some remarkably coincidental relationships. Your fame would come when you wrote an article, titled "Boxometrics," reporting on the selected positive results of your study and ignoring all the negative data.

Maier's Law: If facts do not conform to the theory, they must be disposed of.—N.R.F. MAIER

PYRAMIDOLOGY

The pyramids have been objects of curiosity ever since the Napoleonic invasion impressed the wonders of ancient Egypt on the consciousness of Europe. Napoleon himself was fascinated by what were called "The Mountains of the Pharaohs." He once spent the night in the confines of the Great Pyramid of Giza, emerging pale and shaken the next morning. He refused to disclose details of what caused his fright and ordered that the subject never be mentioned. Many years later at St. Helena, shortly before his death, Napoleon spoke of that event, saying that he had foreseen his destiny. But then he abruptly dismissed the subject again with "You'd never believe me."

Pyramid enthusiasts award great significance to the fact that Alexander Graham Bell worked and conducted his experiments in a laboratory topped with a roof formed in the shape of a pyramid.

Pyramid trivialists note that a pyramid contains more stones than all the cathedrals and churches erected in England since the birth of Christ.

Many volumes have been written that attribute secrets, scientific functions, and mystical powers to the Great Pyramid and claim it to be an architectural revelation for those equipped with a good measuring tape and the ability to interpret their findings.* Dead men tell no tales, but their monuments can intrigue the living.

---

*Some of the mystical powers and revelations attributed to the Great Pyramid are:

    —The ratio of height to width of the pyramid has been calculated to be the time between Adam and Jesus in years.

    —The pyramid is a repository of an ancient and possibly universal system of weights and measures, the model for the most sensible system of space and time measurements available on earth, based on the polar axis of rotation.

Faith Can Move Mountains

Guards discovered a pyramidologist chipping away the stones at a turn in a passage of the Great Pyramid. He was engaged in modifying the pyramid so that it would more accurately fit the mathematical formula he was proposing.

Spinoza's Law: If facts conflict with a theory, either the theory must be changed or the facts.

—BENEDICT SPINOZA

Does the Great Pyramid of Cheops enshrine a lost science? Was this last remaining of the Seven Wonders of the World . . . designed by mysterious architects who had a deeper knowledge of the secrets of this universe than those who followed them?

—PETER TOMKINS,
SECRETS OF THE GREAT PYRAMID

—The main chamber of the pyramid incorporates the "sacred" $3-4-5$ ($a^2 + b^2 + c^2$) and $2-\sqrt{5}-3$ triangles which were to make Pythagoras famous, and which Plato claimed were the building blocks of the cosmos.

—The pyramid was designed on a basis of Hermetic geometry, which was known only to a secret society.

—The pyramid was a theodolite, an instrument of great precision for the surveyor.

—The pyramid was an almanac by means of which the length of the year, including the awkward .2422 fraction of a day, could be measured accurately.

—The pyramid foundation is oriented to true north.

POPULAR PANACEA

Interest in the mystical and therapeutic powers of pyramids appears to come in waves. At one time it is prophecy based on pyramid dimensions that captures public attention, and at another it is the curse of the pyramid or its magic spells. The recent wave of interest in pyramid power, focusing on its preservative and curative energies, seems to have peaked, but its hold on the mind endures.

> I respect faith, but doubt is what gets you an education.
>   —WILSON MIZNER

A Prague radio engineer, Karel Drbal, conducted an experiment to check on a pyramid's ability to dehydrate and preserve the bodies of dead animals. He tried putting a blunt razor blade under one of his model pyramids and reported that the blade became sharp. He shaved with the sharpened blade until it became blunt again, and once more placed it under the pyramid. It became sharp again. Drbal tried to patent and market his discovery. The Prague patent office refused to consider it until its chief scientist built a model pyramid for himself. It worked. Thus the Cheops Pyramid Razor Blade Sharpener (named after the builder of the Great Pyramid of Giza) was registered in 1959 under Czechoslovakian Republic Patent number 91304. A factory soon began to turn out miniature cardboard pyramids. In America the idea caught on and the cardboard-pyramid manufacturing business thrived.

> The true scientist never loses the faculty of amusement. It is the essence of his being.
>   —J. ROBERT OPPENHEIMER

Pyramidologists claim that the same energy that sharpens razor blades can be obtained quickly and easily by anyone, and that it provides practical help for people, animals, plants, and things. It can strengthen, energize, and rejuvenate the body and increase extrasensory perception. Proponents claim that stress-related conditions, such as insomnia, chronic headaches, fatigue, and low back pain, can all be cured by sitting inside a pyramid. Those interested in the economics of pyramid power claim to be justly rewarded too. It can enhance the flavor of less expensive wine and other products, tenderize meat, remove the bitterness from coffee, and dehydrate and preserve foods.

> I kept my jokes under a pyramid to make them funnier. It didn't sharpen the jokes but in removing them I got a nasty paper cut.   —LOTUS WEINSTOCK

PYRAMIDAL PARADIGM

So far, we have discussed the origins of faith in the power of pyramids. Now we will examine the pyramid's influence on us all, no matter what our system of belief.

Translation of Ed. C. Scrolls

SCRIBE: Oh! mighty Pharaoh, you have no peer amid these people.
PHARAOH: Peer amid, Pyramid! That's a great name for the pointy pile of rocks we're building.

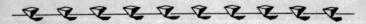

All down the ages mankind has sought a panacea for the world's ills and hoped for some super leader to arise who would lead humanity into utopia, whether by politics, military power, science, philosophy or religion. The Great Pyramid of Giza enshrines the solution to the problem and reveals the only power adequate to put the world right—so completely right as to cause God's will to be done on earth as it is in heaven.   —ADAM RUTHERFORD, *in* Pyramidology, Book II The Glory of Christ as Revealed by the Great Pyramid, *The Institute of Pyramidology, Hertfordshire, Great Britain, 1962*

> History: An account mostly false, of events mostly un-
> important, which are brought about by rulers mostly
> knaves, and soldiers mostly fools. —AMBROSE BIERCE

THE FEUDAL SYSTEM

Early in the development of social order the pyramid
became the model for administration. During the period of
medieval feudalism in Western Europe, the pyramid
evolved into an elaborate formalized administrative structure. At the top was the king, queen, or emperor, who
(theoretically at least) owned all the land. Next came the
hierarchy of nobles, the upper level of which contained the
overlords who held land granted directly by the monarch.
Land of the lesser nobles was granted from their overlords.
Vassals were allotted property by the lesser nobles. Vassals
tilled the land and shared the crops with the landlords, who
shared them with the monarch. Sometimes a land-holding
vassal granted land privileges to another vassal, thereby becoming his lord. Through this process the pyramid became
a ladder of upward mobility within a class society. But no
matter how complex the system became, it never deviated
from its pyramidal structure.

> Every civilization is, among other things, an arrange-
> ment for domesticating the passions and settling them
> to do useful work.   —ALDOUS HUXLEY

THE ROMAN CATHOLIC CHURCH

The longest-enduring administrative hierarchy still in
existence is that of the Roman Catholic Church. Its general
organization starts with the "visual head," the pope (Jesus

Christ is the invisible head). The next stratum down is occupied by the cardinals, who are appointed by the pope.
The cardinals, in turn, upon the death of the pope, elect his
successor. Bishops come next in order of importance.
Priests or pastors form the base of the ecclesiastical pyramid. This organization of the clergy is supported by the
flock, or laity, who form the base of the pyramid.

The operation of this pyramid is intricate and complex,
and beyond the scope of this chapter. The abbreviated description above leaves out the levels within the major
strata, such as archbishops, ordinary bishops, auxiliary
bishops, and so forth, but it is adequate to illustrate the
pyramid principle of the organization.

> It often happens that I wake at night and begin to
> think about a serious problem and decide I must tell
> the Pope about it. Then I wake up completely and
> remember that I am the Pope. —POPE JOHN XXIII

THE MODERN ORGANIZATION

Today there are many theories of administration, and
there is a wide variety of management innovations, but the
basic structure of administrative charts is still the pyramid.
The apex of the business chart is occupied by the chief executive. The next level contains the vice-presidents in
charge of such areas as sales, production, research and development, and administration. The next level is middle
management and consists of the department heads operating within each division. Below the management level is the
supervisory staff, who is the direct administrative authority
over the employees who carry out direct services for the
customers, operate the machinery that produces the product, or do the actual physical work.

Feudal Pyramid

Roman Catholic Pyramid

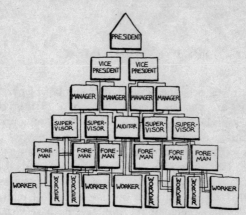

Modern Administrative Pyramid

Virtually every man, woman, and teenager in America owns a miniature pyramid. Remove a $1.00 bill from your wallet and flip it over. Imprinted there is a reproduction of the reverse side of the Great Seal of the U.S.—a pyramid of 13 courses, representing the original 13 colonies, watched over by the Eye of Providence.
— THE PYRAMID RESEARCH FOUNDATION

> In the business world an executive knows something
> about everything, a technician knows everything about
> something—and the switchboard operator knows ev-
> erything.   —HAROLD COFFIN

THE PYRAMIDAL IMPACT

Each of us occupies a place in a number of pyramids.
Most of us are part of the taxpaying base of the governmental pyramid, the apex of which is the occupant of the
White House. As customers of various commercial establishments we are the economic base of the marketing pyramids. As employees we occupy various levels of the
pyramids in which we work, and if we own a business, our
pyramidal status depends on our percentage of interest in
the firm. Each branch of the military, each service club,
lodge, benevolent association, educational establishment,
religious institution, or political party is a pyramidal organization. In spite of the demise of the authoritarian family
structure, there is no family in which leadership, money,
and ability are equally distributed among all members.
Usually the adults have a dominant role with one of the
parents assuming more authority than the other. Thus we
are all occupants of pyramids from cradle to grave.

So it goes. In every aspect of our lives we occupy various positions within the pyramids of which we are a part
while we are controlled by society's organizational pyramids. We are amazed at the durability of the pyramid as a
monumental structure and as a concept for social organization. We are impressed with the mechanical strength and
stability of the pyramid as a geometrical form and are af-
fected by our belief or nonbelief in its mystique as a symbol
of divine power.

Poor Bronsky, he's a little more than halfway finished with building his pyramid. But I don't think he'll ever finish it all the way to the top. You see, the more successful he is, the bigger he wants to build the bottom of the pyramid. And the bigger he builds the bottom, the farther it is to the top. Frankly, if he ever felt he could reach the top of it he'd never start building it in the first place.

—MEL BROOKS to Paul D. Zimmerman
over a pretty good piece of fish at Factor's Deli

2

Peter Pyramid

An apple a day used to keep the doctor away, but not today
because he doesn't make house calls anymore.

—Anon Amos

Although it is not a mistake to believe that pyramids have
great influence in our lives, we have overlooked an important point. Theoretical organizations or administration
charts are based on the base-down or Egyptian pyramid;
whereas the operational pyramid by which we try to get
things done in our everyday lives is a base-up pyramid resting on its point.

   We will begin our exploration of this phenomenon with
a brief example of how the base-up pyramid works.

> All human history attests
> That happiness for man—the hungry sinner!—
> Since Eve ate apples, much depends on
>   dinner.   —Lord Byron

A TEMPTING IDEA

   In the beginning, in the Garden of Eden, Adam and
Eve had direct access to apples. All they had to do was

reach up and pick the alluring fruit. The consequences of falling for this temptation led to serious complications, but for the moment our concern is only with the problem of access to apples.

> It is not the apple on the tree but the pair on the ground that caused the trouble. —M. D. O'CONNOR

Following expulsion from the garden, Adam and Eve were condemned to go to work. Their first job was to scout around and locate trees bearing apples, since they no longer had those that grew around them in the Garden of Eden. Their access to apples, now complicated by travel, was still a relatively simple matter, although it required considerable effort.

> Adam was but human—this explains it all. He did not want the apple for the apple's sake, he wanted it only because it was forbidden.   —MARK TWAIN

Later in the march toward civilization, those not wanting to take a hike every time they desired an apple hit upon the idea of organizing apple-gathering jaunts, bringing back quantities of the fruit to their huts or caves. Once people discovered that the seeds they spit out in their front yards grew into trees bearing apples, the development of agribusiness was inevitable.

> The agricultural population, says Cato, produces the bravest men, the most valiant soldiers, and a class of citizens the least given of all to evil designs.
> —PLINY THE ELDER (Gaius Plinius Secundus),
> A.D. 23–79

Where the apple reddens
Never pry—
Lest we lose our Edens,
Eve and I.
—ROBERT BROWNING

THE SYSTEM ESCALATES

Today, although apples still grow on trees, we get them from the supermarket, where the apple you select was grown by a fruit farmer. It was plucked from its branch by a fruit picker. It was transported to a processing plant by a fruit hauler. It was processed by a number of persons, including graders, packers, and inspectors. It was moved to a storage facility. It was trucked across the country to a produce wholesaler. It then entered the retail system and eventually arrived on the produce counter, where it finally was available—plucked, packed, processed, and "ready for" purchase.

> And pluck till time and times are done
> The silver apples of the moon,
> The golden apples of the sun.
> —WILLIAM BUTLER YEATS

LOST IN THE TRANSLATION

Back down nearer the point of the pyramid, if you hankered after a fresh, ripe apple you could step out the back door and wander down to the orchard, where you could select and pick one right off the tree—ripe, crisp, juicy. There was no one between you and the apple.

Later on, a little farther from the tip of the pyramid, the apple you bought directly from the farmer was usually either a fresh-picked summer apple or a winter apple that had been stored in a root cellar. Often the farmer himself was the only person involved in getting the apple to you. If you bought the apple at your neighborhood grocery, it came from an orchard close to the store. The farmer delivered apples in bushel baskets when he made his trips to market. The summer apples were not as fresh as those directly off the tree, but they were still crisp, juicy, and delicious even though they had passed through several hands before they reached yours.

The apple you buy today has a totally different history. From the tree, it is sent to a controlled-atmosphere storage facility, where the ripening process is inhibited by reduced temperature and chemical treatments. It then travels by refrigerated railroad car or truck to a specialized distribution center. It may then be ripened by exposure to chemicals and enzymes. What emerges from this process is called a fresh apple, but its flavor, crispness, and feel bear little resemblance to the apple you bought from the farmer nearer the point of the pyramid.

INFINITY

Now there is a whole army of people, between the farmer and you, who handle your apple or operate the machinery that handles it. State and federal governments provide a network of subsidies, price controls, import-export regulations, interstate restrictions on movement and sale of fruit, and so forth. The Army Corps of Engineers and other government departments and agencies are involved in the hydro projects that supply water to irrigate the orchards in more arid areas. Government agencies also control the types and quantities of pesticides and other chemicals used in the production of the fruit, as well as chemicals that prevent spoilage and control the ripening. The petroleum companies, prime producers of the chemicals used as pesticides

All organizations are at least 50 percent waste—waste people, waste effort, waste space, and waste time.

—ROBERT TOWNSEND

and fertilizers, come under similar government agency control.

The apple is hauled in a truck driven by an individual who belongs to the 2.3-million-member Teamsters Union. Similarly, each worker who handles your apple—picker, packer, processor, produce manager, and retail clerk—is a member of a union. The store that sells you the apple may be one outlet in a chain of supermarkets that is a subsidiary of a retail-marketing corporation acquired as part of a diversification program by an international corporation.

This is a far from complete look at the Peter Pyramid and how it functions, but it reveals that the process of getting the apple from the tree to you requires thousands of people to pick, process, transport, store, and sell the apple. Thousands more are needed to advertise, merchandise, package, and provide chemicals. Millions of others are connected with them through unions, professional organizations, and government bodies.

> We are anthill men upon an anthill world.
> —RAY BRADBURY

Although the purpose of this inverted pyramid is simply to get an apple from the tree to you, it is an extremely complex system. This makes it difficult to understand the total picture. The processes within the system are so mystifying that great institutions of research and learning devote vast amounts of time, money, and talent to their study. Departments of agriculture, transportation, business administration, law, economics, marketing, and systems engineering study the problems. They teach their specialized answers to students earning degrees and professional certification as agriculturists, lawyers, accountants, engineers, and so forth, who then work in various divisions within the pyramid. This specialization contributes to stratification and categorization of employees and makes change within the system increasingly difficult, with one exception—it is always possible to make things more complex.

> The simple belief in automatic material progress by means of scientific discovery is a tragic myth of our age.   —SIR BERNARD LOVELL

Another problem with the base-up pyramid is that the more it grows, the more unstable it becomes. A malfunction in any component can disturb the total system or bring the whole operation to a stop, even though there are plenty of apples on the trees and the demand for them continues. A strike of agricultural workers could result in the apples not being picked. A shortage of apple boxes could put a hitch in the apple delivery system. As in any complex mechanism, the more components, the greater the opportunity for a part of the system to fail.

My nephew, Peter Lucht, was shopping in a supermarket in Vancouver, British Columbia, when it was announced that nothing could be purchased because the computer had shut down and the store would have to be closed for an undetermined period. Customers abandoned their shopping carts and the clerks immediately went to work returning the merchandise to the shelves. Here the intricate system for getting the apple from tree to consumer failed completely because of a malfunction in the final step. A tiny problem in the computer closed down the cash registers. The store was forced out of

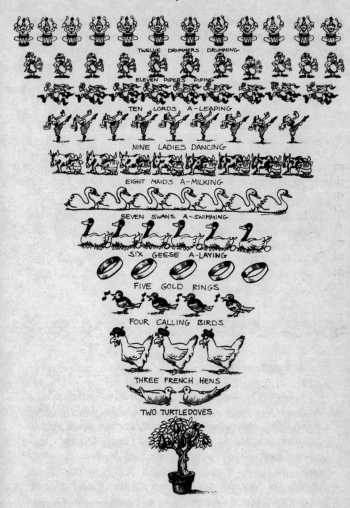

TWELVE DRUMMERS DRUMMING

ELEVEN PIPERS PIPING

TEN LORDS A-LEAPING

NINE LADIES DANCING

EIGHT MAIDS A-MILKING

SEVEN SWANS A-SWIMMING

SIX GEESE A-LAYING

FIVE GOLD RINGS

FOUR CALLING BIRDS

THREE FRENCH HENS

TWO TURTLEDOVES

It is always possible to make things more complex.

business, temporarily, and my nephew could not pur-
chase his apples. A chain is only as strong as its weak-
est link; and the longer the chain, the more weak links.

Attempts are made to keep all parts of the chain
strong and to avoid mishaps like strikes, shortages of
apple boxes, and computer failures. Efforts are also
made to avoid environmental pollution and to eliminate
health hazards in workplaces throughout the apple net-
work. Regulations are made to provide economic sta-
bility to the industry. These attempts to regulate the
system expand its complexity and add to its instability,
producing a top-heavy governmental and private bu-
reaucracy. The system must work because immediate
survival depends on it; therefore, when some part fails,
another component is added to keep it working.

A. Marquet—Grocer

Andy Marquet started in the grocery business as a
delivery boy for his father, and when his father retired
he took over the store. Andy, with the part-time help of
his wife, ran the business. He bought apples, eggs, potatoes, and other produce from the farmers when they
came to town, and they bought their groceries from
Andy. He had almost complete control of his business.

The decisions he made were based on his own experience, intelligence, and judgment of each situation.
He decided on what items to carry. He opened the store

in the morning and closed it at night. He extended credit to regular customers he knew to be reliable. The business was successful. Andy was happy and well respected in the community.

A financier offered to back Andy in a second A. Marquet grocery in a nearby town. He decided to operate the two stores by hiring a clerk for each and by dividing his time between the stores. So the clerks would know what to do in his absence, he made rules. He made rules about purchasing from local farmers. He made rules about requisitions, credit, billing, and all routine matters.

When he acquired the third store, Andy found that he could spend very little time in the stores, so he tried to control the business through more regulations and through a records system that would tell him what was going on in his stores.

Although the inventories, requisitions, and receipts were helpful they did not tell him about what was actually happening when a customer came into a store. When he became aware of problems, he made more rules. He tried to play safe by covering every contingency.

As the chain grew, the stores became standardized. All carried the same products and all had the same layout, the same advertisements, the same rules, and the same red tape. The stores now bought apples, eggs, and potatoes from one central wholesaler. Even store number one, in the heart of apple-growing country, received its apples from a distant supplier.

Back near the beginning, Andy was in the grocery business. He did all the paperwork during the infrequent quiet periods in his thriving business. As his business developed into a working bureaucracy, he had less and less to do with groceries and more and more to do with paperwork. Most of the people who work for him now are not in the grocery business, but are rule makers, rule enforcers, and rule followers. The rules and regulations have become more important than the people and the products.

THE EIGHTH WONDER

The whole pyramid, however, is with us today. Down near the tip there are still primitive peoples in remote areas of Africa and Australia who do not cultivate the land and survive by simply gathering food as nature supplies it. There are still persons of an independent turn of mind who pick apples for their own consumption from their own trees in their own gardens. There are still those who buy their apples directly from growers or barter for them. Some country stores and roadside stands still get apples directly from the farmer. However, the bulk of the apple business is conducted through "regular channels," occupying the highest and largest part of the pyramid.

> Man transforms everything he encounters into a tool;
> and in doing so he himself becomes a tool. But if he
> asks, a tool for what, there is no answer.
> —PAUL TILLICH

THIS END UP

The Peter Pyramid is not simply the Egyptian pyramid inverted. The ancient pyramid, no matter how big its base, eventually comes to a point and that is as far as it can go. The base-up pyramid starts small but inherently has no concluding place. It will never stop by being completed. Because it is not self-limiting, it must grow until it topples over, begins to crumble, self-destructs, or until the people who are building it take action to control its growth.

Each crisis or problem within the system demands a response. But since everything is interlocked in the system, each response affects more than the problem it was meant to solve; each solution creates another problem. As solutions and problems and solutions proliferate, the Peter Pyramid grows layer upon layer.

> How many apples fell on Newton's head before he took the hint! Nature is always hinting at us. It hints over and over again. And suddenly we take the hint.
> —ROBERT FROST

WHO IS TO BLAME?

There is no reason to assume that any of the persons concerned in creating this sort of complicated mess are motivated by evil intentions. In the case of the apple system, the evidence even suggests that many of those involved had the best of humanistic motives. Throughout the ages apples have been credited with possessing health-giving properties. Therefore, increased production and distribution of apples not only help stave off a crisis of hunger among the poor, but also promote health and well-being. An improvement in the health of millions of undernourished citizens makes them better workers, consumers, and taxpayers while preventing them from fomenting social unrest. These advantages justify such government programs as agricultural subsidies to increase production, and food stamps to assure distribution to the poor.

Corporate agriculture's response to the subsidies is as expected. It grows more apples. This requires more energy to power modern farm equipment, and an increased use of fertilizers and pesticides. Transportation of these products to the farms and of the apples to the market necessitates a similar increase in petroleum use, adding to the energy crisis and driving up fuel costs.

Urge-to-Merge Case 980376

Jack B. Nimble, owner of the Nimble Running Shoe Company, and Byron U. Thomson, founder of the B.U.T. Mattress Company, decided that it would be economically advantageous for their companies to merge. Stock in their new organization, Amalgamated Enterprises, had a brisk sale, so they were able to acquire stock in C. Wright Contact Lenses and the controlling interest of Irwin Blight Construction Company. With the increased stock of the expanded Amalgamated holdings, Nimble and Thomson made a bid to take over C. D. Clothing, offering the C. D. stockholders two shares of Amalgamated for every three shares of C. D. Once the agreement was concluded, they were able to float a bank loan to buy the Schwindal Real Estate and Development Corporation.

Using the stocks and credit of the Schwindal Corporation, they made a bid for an interest in Ben E. Fishell Tobacco Products. The contracts granted Ben E. Fishell were adequate collateral for Amalgamated to add Adam's Apple Products to its corporate structure.

*And that is how a running-shoe manufacturer and a
mattress maker who knew nothing about agriculture
ended up owning an apple orchard.*

Federal policy supports the corporate farm over the
communal or individual farm, apparently on the assump-
tion that the big agribusiness enterprise is more efficient,
more productive, and more cost-effective. Ironically research, including that of the U.S. Department of Agriculture, indicates that most of the economic advantages
associated with size can be achieved on the small farm.

> Now as I was young and easy under the
> apple boughs
> About the lilting house and happy as the
> grass was green.   —DYLAN THOMAS

Those who create the corporations are primarily urban
people who regard land, and all that grows on it, as they do
any other component of production. They have positive
feelings about turning traditional farming into a highly specialized agri-industry, leaving less room and little need for
the resident farmers, who then migrate to and populate the
cities to the point of chronic crisis. The sense of personal
satisfaction and family involvement is lost when the farm
family is uprooted from the soil and tries to put down roots
in the concrete of the cities.

Agri-industry production methods mean more expensive machinery, higher wages, and rising costs for fertilizers
and other chemicals. These, plus the increases in the costs
of distribution, put the apples out of the price range of
those needing them the most.

> You can't expect to win unless you know why you
> lose.   —BENJAMIN LIPSON

Pesticides, broadly distributed by crop dusting, contaminate the fruit, pollute the air, and drift on the wind to poison other crops and endanger the health of nearby residents and workers. This hazard, along with the poisoning of the soil, cause increased debilitation and illness, especially among the poor, making many of these people unemployable and limiting their purchasing power, particularly for expensive food items such as the newly priced apples. This swells the need for the food-subsidy program, further escalating its cost.

The increased use of chemical fertilizers means more strip mining for phosphates and other minerals, which in turn destroys more land and releases radioactive particles and other pollutants into the atmosphere. The chemical fertilizers penetrate the soil and eventually leach into the natural water systems to damage fish and other marine life, thereby reducing the supply of edible fish. As this pyramid expands, human health is further endangered and costs spiral upward.

> One weakness of our age is our apparent inability to
> distinguish our needs from our greeds.
>   —DON ROBINSON

THE OLD-FASHIONED WAY

Nature tends to operate self-adjusting, self-cleansing, balanced recycling systems. Sometimes human intervention works in close harmony with these natural systems.

The Peter Pyramid grows layer upon layer

> Great mother of apples it is a pretty world.
> —KENNETH PATCHEN

Back nearer the point of the pyramid, a closed eco-system existed. Horses provided much of the power used on the farm. They were fed, in large measure, from feed grown on that farm, including fallen apples and the grass growing between the fruit trees. A cycle was completed when the animals' manure was used to fertilize the orchard. Even the nutrients from human waste, through the use of septic tanks or other simple sanitation systems, were retained in the immediate area.

> Let us permit nature to have her way; she understands
> her business better than we do.
> —MICHEL DE MONTAIGNE

This ecosystem has been replaced by technology that fertilizes the orchard with chemicals transported over great distances. The apples are themselves transported to far-away cities. The waste products derived from eating the apples are flushed away and poured into rivers and oceans. The ecological loop has been broken and replaced by an energy-intensive, highly exhaustive system. As capital expenditures for farming increase, the small and marginal farmer is squeezed out to join the working poor or the welfare rolls. This adds to government spending, taxation, and inflation that drives the price of apples still higher.

> More will mean worse.   —KINGSLEY AMIS

Within the structure and influence of the Peter Pyramid there is not much that can be done to relieve the situation. Small-farm subsidies from the federal treasury would further increase inflation; and if a ceiling price were imposed there would be a cutback in apple production. The pyramid seems to provide no solution that would get more apples to the underfed, except through increases in the welfare system.

> Progress is man's ability to complicate simplicity.
> —THOR HEYERDAHL

Even though apples may never be rationed directly, the petroleum on which the apple business is so dependent has been in short supply, and may be again. When the crises of oil depletion, OPEC control, and misallocation become acute, the federal government intervenes with a variety of energy proposals, including rationing. Every solution involves more centralized control. To enforce rationing or conservation, a full range of technological solutions and authoritative measures is brought to bear on the problems of allocation and distribution. This produces an expanded Washington bureaucracy, the nature of which is always cumbersome, inefficient, unresponsive, and time-consuming. Tighter control over energy production and use means a greater role for government bureaucrats in extracting, distributing, and marketing. Increased government interference in such formerly private concerns as how fuel is used in industry, on the farm, or in the home causes resistance. Special-interest groups mobilize government lobbies, leading to misallocation of supplies. The overall inefficiencies and misuse of energy and other resources lead to their hastened depletion and drastically impede the production, processing, and delivering of apples.

> I tell you folks, all politics is applesauce.
> —WILL ROGERS

THE PETER PYRAMID PRINCIPLE

In the example presented in this chapter and in all the case studies that follow, you will see that the inverted pyramid is capable of infinite expansion and that the simplest task, when subjected to the complexities and red tape of administrative organization, can become extremely complicated, wasteful, and prone to breakdown.

Three Phases of Pyramidal Growth

As an organization passes through various phases of development, its focus centers on different activities.

Service-Centered Phase

Apple City had become the business and shopping center for a large apple-growing area. Tom, Dick, and Mary saw an opportunity to serve the community and establish their own business. Apple City did not have an independent delivery service, and they felt ideally qualified to provide one. Tom had studied accounting and had driven a delivery truck during his college days. Dick was an experienced driver with a mechanical bent and a good knowledge of motor vehicles. Mary had been a dispatcher for a large department store and was also a capable driver.

The three of them, along with a down payment on two delivery trucks, a rented office, and a small advertising budget, were the total assets of Speedy Delivery. They made daily pickups and deliveries for their reg-

*ular commercial customers and special deliveries on re-
quest. Parcels dropped off at the office were delivered
on the next regular route at a fixed low fee. The business thrived. The partners aimed to please. All three
knew the business and could take care of any inquiry or
serve those who came to the counter in the office. They
were fully conscious of their original purpose and main
mission—to provide for the delivery needs of the businesses and citizens of Apple City. They realized their
function was to serve customers—people outside their
organization. Through serving others they served themselves. They were reminded of this constantly because
their every action was in some way a response to external requirements, that is, customer needs.*

*Although Tom, Dick, and Mary each had a spe-
cialized area of responsibility, the trio functioned with
flexibility. Each filled in as needed to provide the best
service. If Mary was on the phone with a customer
when another customer entered the office, Tom would
leave his bookkeeping to help the newcomer. In this
beginning phase the company could be characterized as
a service-centered organization.*

> And honored among wagons I was prince of the apple
> town.   —DYLAN THOMAS

System-Centered Phase

*As business increased, the company expanded its
fleet of trucks and as requests for service came from
farther and farther up Apple Valley, the company extended its service. Deliveries made to other carriers for
further shipment—to the bus depot, truck- and rail-
freight offices, and to the Apple Junction airport at the
other end of Apple Valley—each required a different set*

of forms and current knowledge of rates and packing requirements. As the business grew, personnel and paperwork expanded. An office manager, Rankin Fyle, was employed to improve the organization and supervise the staff. Tom, Dick, and Mary spent an increasing amount of time training the newcomers and answering customer complaints. During this phase, such complaints became their only customer contacts.

Rankin hired an extra or relief clerk because there was always at least one person missing from the office because of illness, personal emergencies, vacation, personal phone calls, trips to the restroom, coffee breaks, medical checkups, and so forth. The office manager made schedules and job descriptions so that everyone knew what his or her job was and so that the internal organization operated smoothly. During this phase, the company could be called a system-centered organization.

Our little systems have their day.
— ALFRED LORD TENNYSON

Administrator-Centered Phase

Tom, Dick, and Mary relied more and more on the Monday morning staff meeting to keep in touch with the various departments of their expanding business. Rankin performed the usual management functions of budgeting, recruitment and allocation of personnel, and cost accounting. Each Friday afternoon he prepared his report for the Monday morning staff meeting. His main concern was that the report please the partners. Rankin's objective, to please his superiors, became adopted by other staff members also. In this

*phase, the organization became primarily concerned
with internal matters. In contrast to the service-centered
phase, when the aim was to please the customer, now
the customer served the company by his patronage and
by submitting to its system of regulations and paperwork. When Pete Moss came to the counter, he had to
fill out elaborate forms and then stand in line with his
parcels and wait his turn. The other clerk was on coffee
break, the relief clerk was in Rankin's office rearranging her vacation schedule, and the other two clerks were
at their desks. One was on the phone trying to negotiate
a better parking space, the other was answering a personal call, and no one seemed concerned about the traffic at the counter.*

*In this phase, flexibility was replaced by regula-
tions and schedules. Stability was favored over ability.
Any exception to the rules might cause confusion farther down the line, or as Rankin would say, "Disrup-
tion of the chain of command." The major fears
appeared to be that internal routine might be disrupted
or that one of the higher-ups might be offended. The
preoccupation with internal functions and administrative sensibilities resulted in resentment of customers—outsiders whose needs might upset the smooth
internal operation of the system. In this mature or final
phase, the company was an administrator-centered organization.*

*At one of the Monday morning meetings, in order
to please Tom, Dick, and Mary, Rankin Fyle suggested
that Speedy Delivery was hardly a fitting name for such
a complex and distinguished organization, and recommended that the founders be identified in the company's
new name. This is why Speedy Delivery is now called
T.D.M. Services.*

It is no accident that daring and innovation wane as an organization grows large and successful . . . this appears to have been the history of men, of industries, of nations, and even of societies and cultures. Success leads to obligation—not the least of which is the obligation to hold what has been won. Therefore, the energies of a man or administration may be absorbed in simply maintaining vested interests. —ALEX BAVELAS

PERVASIVE PETER PYRAMID

Until our ancestors began to cultivate the land, there was little to defend. A tribe that tilled the soil and planted crops expected to reap the harvest. When an individual or a group from another tribe invaded an agricultural plot or attempted to steal the produce, he or they were driven off. The first weapons of defense were hunting clubs, digging sticks, or other primitive agricultural implements.

Agriculture was a big step in our noble experiment of becoming civilized. It led to permanent settlements, restructuring of tribal life, and specialization of individuals into food gatherers, herdsmen, and hunters. We had come a long way on the road to civilization before the creation of military weapons and the establishment of the profession of soldier.

From these humble beginnings we constructed progressively the most pervasive Peter Pyramid the world has ever known. Today our military might is no longer used to defend crops but primarily to defend or enforce political ideologies. Our present stockpile of weapons is capable of destroying civilization by annihilating the human population and altering the atmosphere so drastically that no food crops could grow for decades.

> The world is a puzzle with a peace missing.
> —ORMLY GUMFUDGIN

RAPID GROWTH

The examples of the Peter Pyramid, presented so far, show how through time and effort a pyramid can be built step by step. In the next case we will see how through casting the smallest seed on fertile ground, a pyramid may spring forth.

I had intended to include in this book a description of how to avoid some of the problems caused by the Peter Pyramid. An article, "Heublein Managers Have a Fallback Position," describing a solution to the Peter Principle appeared in the September 28, 1974, issue of *Business Week* magazine. The article told how the Heublein company had developed a technique called the "fallback position" to assure promoted executives, before leaving their old jobs, that they could return to ones of at least equal status if their promotions did not work out. This would prevent the accumulation of deadwood in the executive suites and thus avoid the Peter Principle and inhibit the growth of the Peter Pyramid. It was my intention to include a quote from the article in this book.

Early in 1983, I wrote to *Business Week,* asking permission to reprint the item, enclosing a copy to illustrate specifically the extent of my request.

In a letter dated March 21, 1983, Eleanore M. Geraghty of *Business Week*'s Permissions Department

Through casting the smallest seed on fertile ground, a pyramid may spring forth.

granted me nonexclusive use on a one-time basis for the item in question if I would comply with the following conditions:

1. Payment of a copyright fee of $100. Our invoice is enclosed.
2. The article must be reprinted in its entirety, with no additions, deletions, underlining/scoring or other changes.
3. There must be no advertising or sales promotional material included on the reprint.
4. If you wish to have a company name, logo, or sales office included on the reprint, you must separate this information from the text of the reprint by a line and the abbreviation "ADV" for advertising material below the line.
5. This credit line must be used. "Reprinted from September 28, 1974 issue of *Business Week* by special permission, (c) 1974 by McGraw-Hill, Inc., New York, NY 10020. All rights reserved."

The terms of the agreement appeared generally acceptable, although the irony of having to pay for permission to quote a short piece about the Peter Principle, in which I had been quoted, did not escape me. But there were things that required clarification. First, why had I received an invoice number 243875 from McGraw-Hill Publications Company, owner of *Business Week,* demanding immediate payment of $100, when it is customary in publishing to pay for nonexclusive permissions when you actually use them? I was just starting to write this book and it might be years before publication. I had not even agreed to *Business Week*'s terms and they wanted payment. Second, I wanted to check with my editor, Howard Cady, to make certain that the permission covered my intended use and that it adequately protected me and my publisher, William Morrow and Company, Inc.

In a letter dated March 25, 1983, I outlined my concerns to Howard Cady and requested that he communicate directly with McGraw-Hill Publications Company to see if an agreement satisfactory to me, William Morrow, and *Business Week* could be arrived at.

In a telephone conversation between Howard Cady and Eleanore Geraghty of *Business Week* Permissions it was agreed that payment would be due on publication of this book. A forbidding note entered the conversation when Ms. Geraghty cautioned that although I did not owe McGraw-Hill any money, the billing was already in the computer and would continue. I was advised to "just ignore the invoices."

At that time McGraw-Hill could not locate my original request in which I specified how I intended to use the item to be quoted, so Howard Cady was asked for more information about this.

In a letter dated June 1, 1983, to Eleanore Geraghty, Howard Cady summarized our discussions of my use of the quoted material, and explained it would be set in a box as in the original article and would appear in the concluding chapter of the book.

In a "Past Due Notice" in the amount of $100 and dated June 9, 1983, sent by the Credit Department of McGraw-Hill Publications Company it was brought to my attention that "Prompt payment will insure a good line of credit for your firm."

The invoices continued until I received a notification dated July 28, 1983, from a computer-control and collection corporation called COLLECTRONICS, in which I was informed that my McGraw-Hill account had been turned over to them for collection. COLLECTRONICS gave an address in Hicksville, New York, and a phone number,

609-448-1700, attention Jean Kerrigan. I phoned, but the number had been changed. I tried the new number several times, but it never put me in touch with COL-LECTRONICS or Jean Kerrigan. So I wrote to Jean Kerrigan explaining that I did not owe McGraw-Hill $100 at this time and that she should refer it back to McGraw-Hill.

I got no reply to my letter, but I did receive a Letegram dated August 11, 1983, marked "Urgent Message" from A. Farber of COLLECTRONICS that said, in part:

> Have recommended to McGraw-Hill Publications that a legal action be commenced against you for the amount as stated above plus interest, legal fees and all other fees incidental to the action.

> If McGraw-Hill Publications accepts our recommendation you may be forced to defend this action at your own expense. Failure to defend against an action may result in a default judgement being entered and a sheriff or marshal requested to levy against your assets.

> Unless your payment of the above stated account is received within 72 hours of receipt of this communication, we shall conclude that you are unwilling to make payment and shall be guided accordingly.

Because of the urgent tone of A. Farber's missive and because Howard Cady was on vacation, I phoned Lawrence Hughes, president of William Morrow, and gave him a rundown of what had occurred over the past few months. He suggested that because William Morrow was now a subsidiary of the Hearst Corporation that he would brief Richard Sugarman, an attorney for the Hearst Corporation, on the matter and that I should inform A. Farber of COL-

LECTRONICS of my action. On August 14, 1983, I sent a letter to A. Farber that said, in part:

> I told you that McGraw-Hill is in error, but you persist in threatening me with legal action. This constitutes unjustified harassment.
>
> Through my publisher, William Morrow & Company Ltd., I have informed attorney Richard Sugarman of the Hearst Corporation, 959 8th Ave., New York, NY 10019 to take action to seek damages against you if you persist in this harassment and threats that could harm my reputation and credit rating.

On August 22, 1983, I received a phone call from Jean Kerrigan, who I discovered now was the credit supervisor for McGraw-Hill. She apologized for the billing that had continued following my cancellation of the request for reprint rights. When I explained that I had not cancelled the request for permission, but that an arrangement had been made through Eleanore Geraghty of *Business Week* Permissions to pay upon publication, she denied that any such agreement had been made. At this juncture I was somewhat confused as to why she was apologizing for not honoring an agreement that she claimed did not exist.

During Howard Cady's vacation, Liz Crosby of William Morrow had been carrying on the negotiations with McGraw-Hill Publications in the matter of Laurence Peter and the $100 permission. This fact and my earlier communication to COLLECTRONICS, attention Jean Kerrigan, were acknowledged in a letter dated August 22, 1983, from Jean Kerrigan, Credit Supervisor for McGraw-Hill.

> I must apologize for the fact that you received another letter from Collectronics despite the fact that the above invoice was being cancelled per your note and

also the phone call from Liz Crosby of William Morrow & Co. Ltd.

Please be assured that as of this date, this invoice
has been cancelled and you will not be hearing anything further from McGraw-Hill Publications or Collectronics.

So far, obtaining permission has involved *Business
Week* magazine, the McGraw-Hill Publications Company,
COLLECTRONICS Corporation, William Morrow and
Company, and the Hearst Corporation; it has required sev-
eral dozen letters and memoranda and eight months of
effort; and has engaged the services of Eleanore Geraghty
of *Business Week*'s Permissions Department, McGraw-
Hill's Jean Kerrigan, supervisor of its credit department,
A. Farber and COLLECTRONICS Corporation, Liz
Crosby, editorial assistant, Howard Cady, senior editor,
Lawrence Hughes, president of William Morrow, and Richard Sugarman, attorney for the Hearst Corporation, along
with all the unidentified assistants, secretaries, and computers.

Even with the assurance that matters are now at rest,
the instability of the previous assurances have convinced
me that the risk of starting the pyramid growing again are
too great, so I have decided not to use the quote.

> The hallmark of our age is the tension between re-
> leased aspirations and sluggish institutions.
> —JOHN GARDNER

Throughout my pyramid studies I have seen a constant
principle at work. Procedures that start out simple and effective end up big and inefficient. Programs that start out
small and beautiful end up in a big, tangled, ugly mess.
Plans that start out clear and comprehensible end up invo-
luted and obscure. Projects that start out on a human scale

The Peter Pyramid: Systems start small and grow to occupy all our time and space.

end up as impersonal, cumbersome, inept bureaucracies. The tendency to begin with a simple design that works, which then develops into a complicated, nebulous, impotent structure, needed further delineation and investigation. To help simplify and define this organizational tendency, I have stated it as a straight forward principle: *The Peter Pyramid: Systems start small and grow to occupy all our time and space.*

> If you should put even a little on a little and should do this often, soon this too would become big. —HOMER

3

Proliferating Pathology

My observation is that whenever one person is found adequate to the discharge of a duty by close application thereto,
it is worse executed by two persons, and scarcely done at all
if three or more are employed therein.
                                        —GEORGE WASHINGTON

The *Encyclopaedia Britannica III* describes a bureaucracy
as "a professional corps of officials organized in a pyramidal hierarchy and functioning under impersonal, uniform
rules and procedures."

If the first person who answers the phone cannot answer your question, it is a bureaucracy.
                                        —LYNDON JOHNSON

Bureaucrats constitute the permanent government in
Washington. They operate the courts, the foreign service,
the military, and every other branch of government. They
are civil servants and do not need your vote for their
power.

Government is too big and important to be left to the
politicians.   —CHESTER BOWLES

In the United States, 2.9 million civilians are federal
government employees, 2.3 million are in the armed ser-

71

vices, and 3 million work exclusively for the federal government through defense and similar contracts. This adds up to 8.2 million, or 10 percent of the total work force. Since 1802, the U.S. population has multiplied fifty-five times, while the number of federal employees has multiplied five hundred times.

This is but the tip of the bureaucratic iceberg. In addition to federal employees, another twelve million people work for state and local governments, and yet another four million work exclusively for government in nominally private jobs. All in all, over one quarter of the working people of the nation are employed in the government sector.

Bureaucracy Observed

I can only assume that a "Do Not File" document is in a "Do Not File" file. —SENATOR FRANK CHURCH

Genghis Khan conquered Asia with an army only half the size of New York City's civil service.
—EMANUEL SAVAS

In government and out, there are vast realms of the bureaucracy dedicated to seeking more information, in perpetuity if need be, in order to avoid taking action.
—MEG GREENFIELD

Dealing with the State Department is like watching an elephant become pregnant.
—FRANKLIN D. ROOSEVELT

Bureaucracy is a giant mechanism operated by pyg-
mies.

—HONORÉ DE BALZAC

If there's anything a public servant hates to do it's
something for the public.   —KIN HUBBARD

   The federal employees are involved in carrying out the
laws and regulations of the country. The official list of
rules, available in the Federal Register, is over sixty thousand pages long and takes up over fifteen feet of shelf
space. Like a snowball rolling downhill, it continues to
grow fatter and take up more space all the time. Each year
Congress creates about two hundred more laws, and federal agencies add about seven thousand regulations.
Throughout the rest of the country, other legislative bodies
write six hundred new laws each day. New boards, agencies, departments, commissions, and bureaucracies must
continually be created to administer these millions of rules.
   A seemingly simple change in a federal regulation—
such as the Employee Retirement Income Security Act of
1974, which was intended to provide protection for workers
in small businesses—can ultimately involve the establishment of a bureaucracy employing thousands of persons. In
the case of the Retirement Act, Congress felt that the
workers covered by small private pension plans were inade-
quately protected. The Act that Congress passed ended up
as 247 small-print pages of regulations that were administered by three separate federal agencies. Each of these
agencies added its own set of regulations and established its
own procedures and interpretations. As the paperwork es-
calated, the personnel grew and the bureaucracy swelled.

Many of the companies that had previously had their own pension plans became overwhelmed with the mounting red tape and dropped their programs. The ultimate result was an increased bureaucracy and an expanded staff of civil servants, yet the purpose of the Act was still largely unfulfilled.

Too Big or Too Small, Case Number 9

The community of South Lake, Texas, applied to the Farmers Home Administration for assistance in expanding its water and sewer system. After appropriate study, the officials of the Farmers Home Administration (FHA) told the people of South Lake that their community was too large to qualify for the FHA program. The FHA then told South Lake to apply for assistance to the Department of Housing and Urban Development (HUD). This required a new application with new forms and new information conforming to HUD guidelines. After their bureaucrats had processed the application, HUD officials told South Lake that the community was too small to participate in the HUD program and recommended that South Lake go back to the FHA for assistance. After FHA officials studied the new application, they stated that the problem was worse than when they had received the original application. It seems the community had grown since the FHA had received the original request. South Lake was advised to return to HUD for assistance. HUD told South Lake that it was still too small to qualify for the program and further expressed doubt that South Lake would ever

*qualify unless it first installed a better water and sewer
system.*   —JAMES H. BOREN

The irony is that our country was established for the
prime purpose of preventing this sort of thing from happening. In the Declaration of Independence, Thomas Jeffer-
son, in a bill of particulars against the king of England,
stated, "He has erected a multitude of new offices, and sent
hither swarms of officers to harass our people, and eat out
their substance." The nation born out of a deep revulsion
of an overbearing government is today a prime example of
an overbearing federal bureaucracy so large that even attempts to catalog it fail. Citizens find that they must protect
themselves against their own government by employing
lawyers, accountants, and tax specialists to help them comply with federal laws and regulations. Even these experts
are frequently at a loss to interpret government requirements. Government bureaucracies could be described as
Public Enemy Number One—bloated, wasteful, and insen-
sitive to those they are supposed to serve.

With one in ten working directly for the federal government, it is inevitable that the bureaucratic presence is
increasingly dominant in our lives. One aspect of this presence was reported in a study by the Federal Paperwork
Commission, in which it was determined that the filling out
of various federal forms by individuals and corporations
costs us about $40 billion a year. This is more than is spent
annually by all the elementary and secondary schools in the
country.

I do not rule Russia; ten thousand clerks do.
                              —NICHOLAS I

HANDBOOK OF BUREAUCRATIC INACTION

TEN FAVORITE EVASIVE STEPS

1. You need written approval from above.

2. Not until you've filed an application.

3. That is outside our jurisdiction.

4. We have never done that before.

5 a. Nobody has ever done it.
b. Somebody else tried it.

6. Our department does not do it that way.

7. Submit seven copies and your request will be considered later.

8. You will be informed in due course.

9. That would be a violation of established procedures.

10. We have your application on file.

Government bureaucracy is the perfect model of the Peter Pyramid. At times this may go undetected because the official or theoretical administrative pyramid is a base-down structure. This explains why so many agencies that appear to be viable, on paper, produce such poor results. Frequently, a functional base-up pyramid is developing within the official base-down organization. It is important to keep in mind when reading this chapter on government bureaucracy that similar pyramids exist in religious, business, union, and other nongovernmental organizations, and that this country does not have a monopoly on the base-up pyramid. It can exist in any bureaucracy, regardless of the type of political system.

Animal Husbandry Case Number 57

The Problem:

> Little Boy Blue, come blow your horn;
> The sheep's in the meadow,
> The cow's in the corn.
> Where is the boy who looks after the sheep?
> He's under the haystack fast asleep.

The Washington Directive

In accordance with the act of Congress of June 6, 1923, as amended we have conducted an extensive inquiry into the need for an adequate signal system in meadows and the adjacent territories. The whole matter of stabilizing practices in these areas is being processed

Official structure meets real structure.

*with a view to attaining the objectives as stated in the
directive of July 7.*

*Considering the matter in the overall aspect, it is
the conclusion of our policy committee, following re-
peated hearings, that the following steps are necessary
to restore confidence and maintain morale:*

1. Immediate stimulation of the entire horn-blowing
   project.
2. A study to determine standards with reference to
   the proper number of blasts to be blown when cows
   are in the meadow.
3. A signal system requiring a signal easily distin-
   guishable from the former when the sheep are reported in the corn.
4. Authorization for a complete study of the whole
   farm situation, and a checkup of the bugle crisis,
   with possible freezing of bugle calls at April levels
   in accordance with the so-called Little Haystack
   Formula.
5. A congressional inquiry to ascertain the number of
   meadows in the country, the square miles of corn
   patches, and the wandering habits of sheep and
   cattle.
6. A census to determine how many boys in the country are under a mandate to look after sheep.
7. A study to determine whether these boys are subject to abnormal indolence or excessive slumber.
8. An appropriation of $5 million to provide adequate
   handling of the haystack matter, to assure an adequate distribution of horns, and to take all necessary steps to integrate, codify, and coordinate all
   authorized operations.

For the purpose of keeping our files accurate, will you inform us of your correct name? It appears on our records as L. Boice Blow, Little B. Bloo, and L. Ittle Boybluh.

  U.S. Cow, Sheep & Haystack Administration
      Washington, D.C.

*Source: U.S. Department of Health and Human Services *Training Manual No. 7.*

IN THE BEGINNING

The word "bureau," meaning a department or agency of government, was derived from a type of desk called a *bureau* that first came into use in seventeenth-century France. It was then natural that the desk of the works foreman, where the records for his department were kept, grew to become the Bureau des Oeuvres Publiques, or Bureau of Public Works.

> People who work sitting down get paid more than people who work standing up. —OGDEN NASH

From every foreman's desk a bureau sprang. For purposes of administration, the staff of the bureau were soon organized into hierarchies, and the power of the bureau became known as bureaucracy. The staff of the bureau consisted of nonelected officials called administrators, civil servants, or bureaucrats. In order for the young bureaucracy to survive, inflexible rules and rigid definitions of responsibility were imposed. When jurisdictional disputes arose, new regulations further defining and delineating re-

17th Century Bureau

sponsibility were drafted. Gradually, as the rules and procedures grew, they impeded effective action, but the bureaucratic solution to its own ineffectiveness was always to create more regulations. It was this kind of administrative structure that was imported to the American colonies, and took root and flourished in the New World.

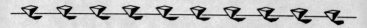

Muddier Mutterings Explained

The following phrases appeared in government statements. Translations were provided by persons from within the respective bureaucracies.

Termination without prejudice—*murder*
Public information strategies on the government's overall response—*official lies*
Detrimental lifestyle behavior—*drinking*
Self-contained breathing apparatus—*gas mask*
Operating within the ambit of guidelines which have previously been established—*carrying on*
A favorable success ratio—*winning*
Irrevocable ramifications for the future—*lasting effects*
Mega-project—*big deal*
Formulate revised proposed objectives and guidelines—*look for new ideas*
Low-density seating—*first class airfare*
Influence of the pricing environment—*cost*
Postpone the immediacy of the implementation—*delay*
Adequate resources to facilitate effective planning over the long term—*money*
Improving the interface—*making friends*
Correction of defects which will have been identified

20ᵗʰ Century Bureau

**during the period between the completion of the specifi-
cations and commencement of the work**—*patching*

BUREAUCRACY TRIUMPHANT

Before I understood how bureaucracies functioned, I
was disturbed when I read a headline: MILLIONAIRE ON
WELFARE!" But after I read the official explanation, I
realized that all was in order. Gary Lashomb, a thirty-one-
year-old supermarket employee, had won New York's mil-
lion-dollar lottery. When he was later laid off from his job,
he applied for unemployment benefits. A state Labor Department official said that lottery winnings were no bar to
receiving such benefits.

> There's only one step from the sublime to the ridicu-
> lous, but there's no road back from the ridiculous to
> the sublime.   —LION FEUCHTWANGER

The Washington Post carried a report of a substantial
study showing that the San Francisco, California, public
schools are more segregated after a $185 million busing
program than before the program began. As long as the
money was spent on busing, in the view of the school system, all was in order.

> When you have a well-constructed state with a well-
> framed legal code, to put incompetent officials in
> charge of administering the code is a waste of good
> laws, and the whole business degenerates into farce.
>   —PLATO

J. Ralph Corbett contributed $160,000 to the city of Cincinnati to build a new music hall, and discovered that it does not pay to be generous. A week later he received a bill from the city for another $6,080. The bill was a service charge for handling the gift. Once again all was in fine bureaucratic order.

While surveying his domain, a newly appointed commissioner of motor vehicles of a midwestern state inquired about one room in which stood rank upon rank of metal file cabinets. He was told that these cabinets held records of all the leases of all the motor vehicles in the state. The files were beautifully kept by a staff dedicated to alphabetization.

The commissioner was impressed by the competence of this branch. He turned to go, but a thought struck him. "What do we do with these records?" he asked. The answer, solemnly supplied as a full explanation, was "Why, we file them."

Further inquiry disclosed that never had a record left the file room; the filing of vehicle leases had no useful purpose whatsoever. Once more we see that bureaucratic order had been valued above purpose.

> You seduced me into that dreadful scientific error: the substitution of important, unanswerable questions for unimportant, answerable ones.
>
> —DONALD KENNEDY,
> on leaving the FDA Commission.

THE BUREAUCRAT

As the bureaucratic pyramid grows, the function of the bureaucrat becomes increasingly difficult to explain to the outsider. Even when the bureaucrat has a title such as coor-

50,000 B.C.   1933

1890

100,000 B.C.   1984

Civilization declines in relation
to the increase in bureaucracy.
— Victor Yannacone

dinator, planner, manager, administrator, processor—a title suggesting some kind of positive action—he may, in fact, be occupied primarily in enforcing or obeying rules, monitoring red tape, shuffling papers, and taking evasive and defensive action.

Note: This was found in the files of a late-departed bureaucrat.

Zen and the Art of Bureaucratic Maintenance

Go placidly amid the noise and the haste and remember what peace there may be in nonresponsiveness. As far as possible, be on good terms with all other bureaucrats. Speak quietly and clearly and listen to others, even the dull and ignorant; they too have information for your files. Avoid loud and aggressive persons, they are vexatious to the bureaucratic spirit. If you concern yourself with others you may become upset and bitter, for always there will be greater and lesser persons and those of superior and inferior status in the hierarchy. Enjoy your power as well as that of your department. Keep interested in your career, however humble; it is your real possession and security in the changing fortunes of time. Exercise caution in your business or department affairs, for the world is full of trickery. But let this not blind you to what virtue there is in tenure, so beware of persons who strive for high ideals, and those full of heroism. Be yourself, but stay within established guidelines. Neither be cynical about rules; for in the

*face of all stupidity and disenchantment, it is regulation
that provides perennial protection. Take kindly the
counsel of the years, gracefully surrendering the ideas
of youth. Conformity, not strength of spirit, will shield
you in sudden misfortune. But do not distress yourself
with imaginings. Many fears are born of boredom, so
involve yourself in the intricate patterns of dysfuntional
complexity. Beyond ritualistic discipline, be gentle with
yourself. You are an inhabitant of the universe, no less
than the trees and the stars: You have a right to be here.
And whether or not it is obvious to you, the universe is
unfolding as it should.*

*Therefore, be at peace with the Bureaucracy, what-
ever you conceive IT to be; and whatever your labors
and aspirations, in the confusion of life, keep peace
with your department. With all its shams, drudgery,
and broken dreams, it is still a beautiful system. Be
content. Strive to be happy.*

Let us take a look at the circumstances that contribute
to the development of the special personality we have come
to know as the bureaucrat.

The person in a beginning-level bureaucratic position
is not usually called upon to show either courage and decisiveness or cowardice and defensiveness. However, as the
individual begins to climb the administrative ladder, certain
personal characteristics are encouraged and rewarded.
Since the first principle of bureaucracy is the bureau's own
survival, high value is placed on the individual's care in
avoiding any action that might embarrass the organization.

Some men are born mediocre, some men achieve mediocrity, and some men have mediocrity thrust upon them.
—JOSEPH HELLER

His tenure, promotions, salary increments, and feeling of belonging, all depend on caution. They are put in jeopardy by independence, decisiveness, or almost any precipitous action.

> The work of internal government has become the task
> of controlling the thousands of fifth-rate men.
> —HENRY ADAMS

If the person tries to cut through the red tape in order to get something done, he is accused of "exceeding his authority," "not following approved procedure," "going over the head of his superior," "operating outside of established guidelines," or in extreme instances, "disloyalty to the department." Whatever the language, clearly he has stuck his neck out dangerously when he has tried to accomplish something.

> It is apparent that many persons wishing to batten on
> the estates of the treasury have devised titles, such as administrators, secretaries, or superintendents, whereby
> they procure no advantages for the treasury but eat up
> the revenues.
> —A ROMAN OFFICIAL, A.D. 288

Under these conditions the true bureaucrats emerge—the hierarchically adjusted men or women. These individuals fit the structure perfectly. They conform to authority and are obsequiously obedient to their superiors in the chain of command, while being authoritative and officious to those with less authority—ultimately, the public.

*It is the anonymous "they," the enigmatic "they" who are in charge. Who is "they"?
I don't know. Nobody knows. Not even "they" themselves.   —JOSEPH HELLER*

Top Ten Excuses

1. I thought it was in the mail.
2. I'm so busy I haven't gotten around to it.
3. I didn't know you were in a hurry for it.
4. You'll have to wait until the supervisor returns.
5. I'm waiting for an OK.
6. That's their job—not mine.
7. No one told me to go ahead.
8. That's not my department.
9. That's the way it's always done here.
10. Just as soon as it clears the review board we'll process your application.

Public servants have greater devotion to the rules, rituals, and records of their departments than to the output of service. Nobody but a bureaucrat likes to be ruled by rules, and nobody but a bureaucrat likes to say, "I don't make the rules, I'm just here to see they are carried out."

> The ultimate bureaucrat is the computer. It is mindless, sexless, heartless, initiativeless, soulless, and finally wisdomless. —SID TAYLOR

Attempts have been made to evaluate the performances of federal bureaucrats, but they are so set in their defensive ways that the evaluations are unproductive. For example, during the 1970s, when civil service annual merit salary increases were based on evaluations, more than 99 percent qualified for increases.

A Government Pay Scale Explained

At the end of two years, the employee will be placed in a lower grade. The employee's pay will be set at the employer's allowable former rate of basic pay or at 150 percent of the highest rate of the grade in which the employee is placed. Following that, the employee will receive 50 percent of any annual comparability increase until the maximum rate for the new grade equals or exceeds the adjusted rate.

— From a Department of Energy publication

If tenure and salary are not dependent on performance, what is there for the bureaucrat to fear? Only one thing—a budget cut affecting the department that could eliminate his job. Survival is dependent on budget, and no activity within any government bureaucracy receives a higher priority than securing a bigger budget.

> Don't ask the barber whether you need a haircut.
> —DANIEL S. GREENBERG

As an agency matures, its concentration on internal operation grows while its enthusiasm over its original purpose wanes, but the only objective that is always pursued with zeal is more funds. Political economy is a contradiction in terms.

> For a ruling bureaucracy, the possession of power is
> the highest goal, and to keep and strengthen its power
> is the paramount aim of its policy. —Erich Strauss

Increased budgets provide for three lines of defense of the status quo: (1) More money means the staff can be increased, bringing aboard new employees with less seniority who will be the first to go in case of a cutback. (2) Since status within a bureaucracy is determined primarily by the number of employees supervised, increases in personnel enhance the bureaucrat's income, rank, security, and ego. (3) Funds also make possible the development of specialized personnel—executive officers, planning analysts, budget directors, administrative officers, congressional liaison officers, public information supervisors, and interagency coordinators—all of whose prime function is to establish a strong funding network for the agency. Money begets money; more money makes it possible to employ more fund-garnering personnel.

> There are hurdles in a society in which one bureaucrat
> engenders not another bureaucrat, but ten bureaucrats, each with his pyramid of power.
> —Han Suyin

Bureaucrats, as a species, are not personally less competent than other groups. Many are intelligent and highly qualified. They work with the best of modern equipment and the latest and most pertinent information, and their pay exceeds that of the private sector. Indeed, we have the best bureaucrats that money can buy. They are especially talented at handling paper. Of the billions of pieces of paper they shuffle every year, each piece must either stay in orbit or arrive on somebody's desk to be signed, rerouted, or filed.

> When a bureaucrat makes a mistake and continues to
> make it, it usually becomes the new policy.
> —JAMES H. BOREN

Bureaucrats are not lazy do-nothings; they are busy people. They attend meetings, write memoranda, plan budgets, organize and reorganize departments, and do many of the other things that administrators of thriving enterprises do; but they do them with a different purpose.

> A committee is a cul-de-sac down which ideas are
> lured and then quietly strangled.
> —SIR BARNETT COCKS

They write memos because writing memos demonstrates that they are busy, and because once written the memos become documented evidence that the writer has been busy. Bureaucrats attend meetings because doing so gives the appearance of importance and useful activity, even if meaningful action is seldom taken. Rushing from meeting to meeting, and particularly traveling great distances to attend meetings, gives the impression that participation is of great importance.

> Meetings are indispensable when you don't want to do
> anything.   —JOHN KENNETH GALBRAITH

A historical event contributing significantly to the timidity and self-protective attitude of federal employees was the loyalty-oath program established in 1947. The significance of requiring the oath was open to a variety of interpretations, but to the already fearful it was a signal for greater conformity. Their fear was heightened by the spectacle of careers ruined and reputations destroyed by the methods of guilt by association or inference used by Senator Joseph McCarthy and the House Committee on Un-

Armadillo (är-maˊdĭlŏ)
burrowing mammal protected
by armored plates.

Bureaucrat (byŏŏə́-krăt)
burrowing mammal protected
by memos, meetings, and
civil service codes.

American Activities. The net result has been a preoccupation with self-protection that far outweighs any instinct for public service.

> It is a commonplace observation that work expands so as to fill the time available for its completion.
> —C. NORTHCOTE PARKINSON

HYPERPOLYSYLLABICOMANIA
(FONDNESS FOR BIG WORDS)

> It is impossible to indoctrinate a superannuated canine in the intricacies of innovative feats of legerdemain.

The desire to impress by using big words is a common and not very harmful trait, but the polysyllabic syndrome from which bureaucrats suffer presents a serious problem for society. Language that was originally developed for communication now serves many purposes. For the bureaucrat it is a primary means of protecting the bureaucracy and himself. Bureaucratic defensive language borrows heavily from lawyer talk or legalese.

> Lawyers spend a great deal of their time shoveling smoke.   —OLIVER WENDELL HOLMES, JR.

Legalese is not only the use of words that are perceived as having legal status, but also it is a way of stringing the words together. If an ordinary man wants to give an apple to another, he merely says, "I give you this apple." But when a lawyer does it, he says it this way: "Know all men by these presents that I hereby give, grant, bargain, sell, release, convey, transfer, and quitclaim all my right, title, interest, benefit, and use whatsoever in, of, and concerning this chattel, otherwise known as an apple or pome fruit of the genus *Malus,* family Rosaceae, together with all the appurtenances thereto of skin, ripened ovary, and surrounding tissue, hereinafter referred to as pulp, seeds, juice, and stem . . ."

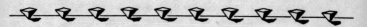

Law and Order

The minute you read something you don't understand, you can almost be sure it was drawn up by a lawyer.
—WILL ROGERS

The United States is the greatest law factory the world has ever known.
—CHIEF JUSTICE CHARLES EVANS HUGHES

Under current law, it is a crime for a private citizen to lie to a government official but not for the government official to lie to the people.   —DONALD M. FRASER

It is on himself that man can inflict the worst punishments.
—ISAAC BASHEVIS SINGER

Man is trampled by the same forces he has created.
—JUANA FRANCES

The human race's prospects of survival were considerably better when we were defenseless against tigers than they are today when we have become defenseless against ourselves.
—ARNOLD TOYNBEE

In days gone by, it was acceptable to "plan" projects, but now bureaucrats "conceptualize, fuctionalize, operationalize, conduct feasibility studies, or research structural constructs." Somehow this officialese, jargon, or gobbledygook is believed to provide a line of defense.

> If you think that you can think about a thing, inextricably attached to something else, without thinking of the thing it is attached to, then you have a legal mind.   —THOMAS REED POWELL

Military spokesmen talk about "limited air interdiction," when they mean bombing; political scientists say "counterfactual propositions," instead of lies, "misspoke" for telling untruths, "destabilization" for the overthrow of foreign governments; safety specialists use words like "impact attenuators," instead of bumpers. Social welfare bureaucrats say "deprived elements," instead of poor people, and "cohabitor" for sex partner, "Human Resources Department" for unemployment office, and "dysfunctional employment patterns" for poor work habits.

> Remember—the tedium is the message.
> —BRIAN ENO

When bureaucrats assemble these types of words into reports, regulations, or memoranda, the outcome can be beyond comprehension.

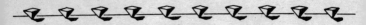

Legalese

Legalese, which may give the impression of errorproof language, is frequently anything but precise.

A memorandum is written not to inform the reader but to protect the writer.
                                                            —DEAN ACHESON

The use of "and/or" was begun because of a difficulty in translating Latin conjunctions into English. In 1894, the first time the legal use of "and/or" was debated, it was given three different interpretations. It has been a consistent cause of misunderstanding to this day. "Aforesaid" is a Middle English word that has contributed to legal babble for hundreds of years. It is used to refer to something that has been said, but is nonspecific as to what it refers to, therefore can lead to a serious misreading. "Whereas" is one of the most utilized and vaguest words in legal writing. It has so many contradictory meanings as to be virtually meaningless. Any word that can mean in one instance "considering that" and in another, "on the contrary" or "the fact is," and the opposite, "in spite of the fact," should be dropped from any responsible person's vocabulary. The ultimate incompetence is that our straightforward agreements and transactions are written up in this kind of jargon.

Bureaucratese lacks eloquence but makes up for it with banality and pomposity. Because it is composed of buzz words and lacks grammatical structure, it is an easy language to speak, but a difficult one to understand.

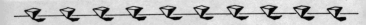

Communication Defined

The cognitive development of any individual organism is functionally dependent on that organism's substantive comprehension of the variables involved in

the dynamic process of symbolic transmission we typically refer to as communication.
—FROM A COURSE AT THE U.S. ARMY LOGISTICS MANAGEMENT CENTER AT FORT LEE, N.J.

Let Me Make That Perfectly Clear

. . . it is proposed that directorate level OPR review and deletion or recertification of essentiality be accomplished on all Air Force publications.
—FROM A DIRECTIVE TITLED *AIR FORCE PROGRAM FOR MAKING DEPARTMENTAL PUBLICATIONS UNDERSTANDABLE BY USERS*

Decision-making Directive

Action-oriented orchestration of innovative inputs, generated by escalation of meaningful indigenous decision-making dialog, focusing on viable urban infrastructure . . .
—U.S. DEPARTMENT OF HOUSING AND URBAN DEVELOPMENT

Two-way Communication

At such a time, the stimulation of transnational linkages necessary for meaningful two-way communication must supersede propagandistic and chauvinistic functions which in the past constituted too large a share of our activities.
—JOSEPH DUFFEY, ASSISTANT SECRETARY OF STATE FOR EDUCATIONAL AND CULTURAL AFFAIRS

Air Fare

If the aggregate amount of claims filed by charter participants under this bond for a single charter trip exceed (without regard to the provisions of this paragraph) the Secured Amount for that trip, the liability of the surety of each charter participant shall not exceed an amount determined by multiplying the Secured Amount by a fraction of the numerator which is the amount for which the security would be liable to the charter participant. —CIVIL AERONAUTICS BOARD

As this incomprehensible language develops, the quantity of words expands so as to become meaningless. Ultimately ideas lose their value. This inverted pyramid of profuse, blunted words grows in volume, but not in content, until it is one huge mass of unintelligible babble.

> Ours is the age of substitutes: instead of language, we have jargon; instead of principles, slogans; and, instead of genuine ideas, bright ideas. —ERIC BENTLEY

In recent years legislators, at the federal level, have made a number of efforts to have bureaucrats write plain or understandable English. Individual citizens have sent incomprehensibly worded regulations and messages back to the agency issuing them, with requests that they be explained in standard English. Another attempt at improvement has been to draw attention to and ridicule the perpetrators of these crimes against our mother tongue.

Senator and Legislature Receive Gobbledygook Award

In California, couples ending their marriage do not have to pay a tax on deeds required in the division of

*their property. This is explained in a new law—Section
11927 of the Revenue and Taxation Code—as follows:*

> (a) Any tax imposed pursuant to this part shall not
> apply with respect to any deed, instrument, or other
> writing which purports to transfer, divide, or allocate
> community, quasi-community or quasi-marital prop-
> erty assets between spouses for the purpose of effect-
> ing a division of community, quasi-community, or
> quasi-marital property which is required by a judg-
> ment decreeing a dissolution of the marriage or legal
> separation, by a judgment of nullity, or by any other
> judgment or order rendered pursuant to Part 5 (com-
> mencing with Section 4000) of Division 4 of the Civil
> Code, or by a written agreement between the spouses,
> executed in contemplation of any such judgment or
> order, whether or not the written agreement is incor-
> porated as part of any of those judgments or orders.
> (b) In order to qualify for the exemption provided in
> subdivision (a) the deed, instrument, or other writing
> shall include a written recital, signed by either spouse,
> stating that the deed, instrument, or other writing is
> entitled to the exemption.

*Introduced by Senator John W. Holmdahl to the
1981 California legislature, it was considered by Pro-
fessor Robert W. Benson's legislation class at Loyola
University Law School as the year's greatest example of
enacted legalese. They awarded it their Certificate of
Expertise in Legal Gobbledygook. They felt both the
legal and communication purposes of the act would be
better served by a plain English version:*

> There is no tax under this Act, when husband and
> wife divide property between themselves because they
> are ending their marriage, or nullifying it, or legally
> separating.

On the document which would otherwise be taxed, husband or wife shall sign a statement saying that this exemption applies.

All efforts to restore bureaucratese to communicative language should be encouraged.

A word fitly spoken is like apples of gold in pictures of silver.   —PROVERBS 25:11

BIGGER IS BIGGER

Bureaucracy on a small scale has been with us for over two hundred years, but the seeds for many of our huge Peter Pyramids were planted during the presidency of Franklin Delano Roosevelt (1933–1945). The boom and excesses of the roaring twenties ended with a thud. On October 29, 1929, President Herbert Hoover declared, "The fundamental business of this country . . . is on a sound and prosperous basis." Four days later the New York stock market crashed. During the remaining three years of Hoover's term, the economic downswing continued. The Great Depression was under way. Twelve million people, one quarter of the entire work force, were unemployed, 5,000 banks failed, 86,000 businesses failed, 273,000 families were evicted from their homes, national income plunged by more than half, from $87.4 billion to $41.7 billion, and most private charities dried up.

In response to this financial stagnation and vast unemployment, Roosevelt started a number of innovative programs. People were put to work on a wide variety of federal projects of significant value to the country. The Works Progress Administration (WPA) built the Lincoln Tunnel connecting New York City to New Jersey, Boulder Dam (renamed Hoover Dam in 1947 to honor ex-President Herbert Hoover), La Guardia Airport, and many other worthwhile enterprises. Each new agency was designed to fulfill Roosevelt's commitment to the economic recovery and stability of America.

> I pledge you, I pledge myself, to a new deal for the American people. Let us all here assembled constitute ourselves prophets of a new order of competence and courage.
> —FRANKLIN D. ROOSEVELT

The New Deal, the Economic Recovery Administration, and Roosevelt's charismatic leadership contributed directly to saving the American way of life. A new spirit of assurance was created that got things moving again. Roosevelt adapted a phrase of Henry David Thoreau's, "Nothing is so much to be feared as fear," and used it in his famous statement ". . . the only thing we have to fear is fear itself." Many who had lost hope were willing to try again. A total collapse was averted and the free-enterprise system survived.

> Even the iron hand of a national dictator is in preference to a paralytic stroke.
> —ALF LANDON, Republican governor of Kansas

The agencies established to accomplish these feats were small and efficient by today's standards. It cost the WPA only $82 to produce a one-man month of employment. The WPA spent 86 cents out of every dollar on wages for people who needed the work, 10.5 cents on material, and only 3.5 cents on administration. It was one of

Roosevelt's beliefs that welfare should be a temporary measure and that recipients should be put to work. Roosevelt was a conservator of traditional values and ways, but he started some of the agencies that have expanded to engulf the nation.

> If we do not halt this steady process of building commissions and regulatory bodies and special legislation like huge inverted pyramids over every one of the simple constitutional provisions, we shall soon be spending billions of dollars more.
>
> —FRANKLIN D. ROOSEVELT

The expansion of bureaucracy accelerated rapidly during World War II, when centralized authority was needed to mobilize the nation. Each succeeding war has had the same effect. Governments expand in times of war, but shrink only slightly in times of peace, so that each war contributes to a larger permanent bureaucracy.

Government bureaucracy has continued to grow under each president since Roosevelt, in spite of oft-repeated promises of cutbacks. During Lyndon Johnson's term of office, government medical insurance was launched, which now costs $57 billion a year—more than eight times the total average annual federal outlay during Roosevelt's first term. Richard Nixon was president when the billion-dollar school lunch program got under way. Jimmy Carter started a project to control bureaucratic growth, but the committee assigned to study the problem got bogged down because there was no accepted or official definition of a government agency and no list of all the agencies. Under these conditions, attempts to differentiate between official government bureaus, joint government and private agencies, organizations operating under government sponsorship, and so forth, were virtually impossible, so little progress was made. President Reagan attempted some cutbacks in education and welfare, while the military bureaucracy and budget advanced rapidly. It appears that pledges to curb bureaucratic growth are still in the promises stage, and that when cutbacks do occur they are offset by growth in other areas.

The federal government has become the single largest entity in the country. This is partly the result of the accelerating expectation of what we want government to do, and partly because of bureaucracy's capacity for autonomous growth. Not only do agencies expand, they multiply. This sometimes comes about through the centralizing and decentralizing phases that bureaucracies go through, like swings of a pendulum. Releasing centralized control allows the decentralized units to develop into full-blown entities, so that each time the central control process is reinstated, the central bureaucracy is bigger than ever. In the process it has spawned a flock of subsidiary bureaucracies, each of which may in time do the same thing.

> We can lick gravity, but sometimes the paperwork is
> overwhelming.   —WERNER VON BRAUN

Government now extends into every aspect of society. The larger and more widespread the bureaucracy, the more wasteful, inefficient, autocratic, and corrupt it becomes and the greater the difficulty in taking any corrective action.

> Amid the seeming confusion of our mysterious world,
> individuals are so nicely adjusted to a system, and sys-
> tems to one another and to a whole, that, by stepping
> aside for a moment, a man exposes himself to a fearful
> risk of losing his place forever.
>   —NATHANIEL HAWTHORNE

The nearest thing to immortality in the world is a government bureau.
—GENERAL HUGH S. JOHNSON

The most obvious difference between government bureaucracies and those of the private sector is that the former are set up to spend money, while most private establishments try to make money. A more subtle difference is that one would have to search for quite a time in the business world to find the equivalent of the Administrative Officer of the United States Government Inter-office Affairs Council on Coordination and Rectification.

> The longer the title, the less important the job.
> —GEORGE McGOVERN

A bureaucracy that enjoys civil service protection and is mired in regulations and overwhelmed with paperwork is particularly difficult to evaluate.

> The inner spirit of bureaucracy lies in the exciting interplay of nonideas and the effervescent sparkling of human personalities engaged in nondirective pursuits.
> —JAMES H. BOREN

Efforts to remove nonfunctional bureaucrats by competency examinations or review boards merely generate new jobs. In many cases the employee's competence or incompetence is irrelevant because the job is useless no matter who is doing it. A genuine bureaucrat looks upon a promotion as a reward rather than as an opportunity for greater accomplishment.

> The great advantage of being in a rut is that when one is in a rut, one knows exactly where one is.
> —ALAN BENNETT

Reorganization orders are often welcomed by bureaucrats. It is a challenge that gives them something to do. Administrative charts are redrawn. New job titles are created with higher grade classifications. Bigger budgets and higher salaries are requested. Buildings are remodeled and office space reassigned. This in itself requires the sharpness of a chess player, since the government owns about a half-million buildings, and leases space in privately or foreign-owned buildings for about $900 million annually.

> Bureaucratic function is sustained by fear of failure as the church was once supported by the fear of damnation.
> —RICHARD N. GOODWIN

Despite reorganization or any other activity inside an agency, not much changes on the outside. Educational standards still decline. Crime still increases. Poverty continues unabated. In other words, while internal reorganization may take place, external inaction remains constant. Some cynics have even suggested that bureaucrats know instinctively that if their agencies corrected the problems they were established to solve, they would do themselves out of a job. It appears that as long as the heads of agencies are responsible for judging their own performance and that of their departments, change is unlikely.

Ask a Silly Question

> The rate per 100 pounds applicable for the transportation of 999 pounds or less, for the applicable mileage, column (a), is that shown in column (b) unless the weight equals or exceeds the number of pounds shown in column (c) for the applicable mileage; in the latter case, the applicable rate is that shown in column (d) for the same mileage, and the applicable weight is the

The Bland Leading the Bland

minimum hundredweight of that column, instead of
the actual weight of the goods transported.
                    —FROM A BULLETIN ISSUED BY THE
                    GENERAL SERVICES ADMINISTRATION

A document issued by the Occupational Safety
and Health Administration (OSHA) reads: "The skin
is an important interface between man and his environment."

The cognitive or mentally evaluative dimension of
such vehicular interactions or potential interactions
was lost in error variance not considered at all in formulations of aerodynamic disturbance functions and
driver performance factors
                    —FROM A STUDY OF
        THE FEDERAL HIGHWAY ADMINISTRATION TITLED
        MOTORIST ATTITUDES TOWARD LARGE TRUCKS

I have condensed my study of bureaucrats and bureaucracies into ten observations.

PETER'S BUREAUCRATIC PRINCIPLES

1. The bureaucracy must be protected.
2. Bureaucratic survival is contingent on an increased
   budget.
3. Bureaucracies breed.
4. Bureaucracies avoid doing anything for the first time.
5. Large bureaucracies grow from small ones, but do not
   perform the functions for which they were initially established.

6. Bureaucracies attract a type of personality adapted to thrive in them.
7. Bureaucracies value internal harmony over output or service.
8. Bureaucracies defend the status quo long past the time the quo has lost its status.
9. An individual with real leadership ability wanting to become a bureaucrat is as likely as a competent jockey wanting to become a horse.
10. In an emergency a bureaucracy will offer you every assistance short of help.

> The pyramids are solidly built, have a nice view from the top, and serve as a resting place for the dead.
> —GERALD A. MICHAELSON

4

Progressive Processes

Millions are fascinated by the plan to transform the whole world into a bureau, to make everybody a bureaucrat, to wipe out any private initiative. The paradise of the future is visualized as an all-embracing bureaucratic apparatus . . . Streams of blood have been shed for the realization of this idea.
—LUDWIG EDLER VON MISES

So far I have discussed negative characteristics of the Peter Pyramid. Now let us examine some of its positive qualities and question its potential for betterment of the human condition. Many of our greatest achievements could have been accomplished only through the sequential development of what have become complex processes. Many great contemporary scientific discoveries could not have been made had not primitive man started the ball rolling through simple curiosity about his environment. One discovery has led to another until today we have detailed knowledge of the structure of a single cell and of the whole solar system.

The stumbling way in which even the ablest of scientists in every generation have had to fight through thickets of erroneous observations, misleading generalizations, inadequate formulations and unconscious prejudice is rarely appreciated by those who obtain their scientific knowledge from textbooks.
—JAMES B. CONANT

Anthropologists tell us that our ancestors lived in trees but, seeing the opportunity to improve their lot, they gave it up for a nomadic terrestrial existence. When the advantages of this more adventurous lifestyle palled, they sought the security of a permanent address and became cave dwellers. Still later, not content with the substantially improved comfort of cave living, they gave up the shelter of the cave in favor of communities of huts built from mud or grass, in locations of popular choice. As time passed, our ancestors' tendency to discontent produced a series of improvements, so that huts became houses and constructing them became a specialty. The professions of architect, mason, carpenter, plumber, and city planner were born. Great and beautiful structures became a preoccupation that eventually resulted in the Parthenon and the Empire State Building. But even a 102-story, 1,250-foot-tall structure was still not enough, and buildings have since been constructed that are even taller.

> If there is technological advance without social advance, there is, almost automatically, an increase in human misery. —MICHAEL HARRINGTON

It is our perpetual discontent, which comes partly from a spirit of adventure and a longing to learn more, that has produced all human progress. Man in space would be an impossibility without a long history of dissatisfaction with our accomplishments, whatever they might be at any particular time. The first step toward space exploration was taken when our ancestors began to walk upright. Sequentially we progressed to wearing shoes, then to riding beasts of burden, horse-drawn vehicles, bicycles, trains, automobiles, airplanes, supersonic jets, and space capsules.

The lower levels of the base-up pyramid have remained intact as we constructed the upper levels. In this

Man has always been an explorer. There's a fascination in thrusting out and going to new places. It is like going through a door because you find the door in front of you. I think that man loses something if he has the option to go to the moon and does not take it.

—NEIL ARMSTRONG

The larger the island of knowledge, the longer the shoreline of wonder.
—RALPH SOCKMAN

space age there are still primitive people walking barefoot while others wear shoes, ride horses, pedal bicycles, board trains, drive cars, fly planes, or rocket into space.

> Man has pursued a lot of dreams—the golden fleece, the alchemist's stone and the idea that the car can be packed for a family vacation so that only one suitcase need be brought into the motel at night.
> —BILL VAUGHAN

IS IGNORANCE INCREASING?

Clearly, some Peter Pyramids are an inevitable outcome of progress. In the early days of our existence we had no knowledge of anything beyond the immediate environment. Human knowledge was like a tiny island in a vast sea of ignorance. As our ancestors began to investigate their environment, they expanded the boundary of their knowledge and understanding. This expanding boundary exposed them to increasing contact with the unknown.

> All we know is still infinitely less than all that remains unknown. —WILLIAM HARVEY

Our awareness of our ignorance occurs at the point at which our knowledge runs out. As we move the boundary of knowledge forward and the boundary of ignorance back, each answer uncovers at least two more questions. Seeing no end to this process, we must conclude that what is unknown is infinite. The more that is known, the longer the line of confrontation between the known and the unknown. Everything we learn increases our ignorance.

COMMUNISM OR CAPITALISM?

The Peter Pyramid operates in both socialist and capitalist societies. The initial establishment of socialistic or communistic political systems requires great creativity, because of the need for detailed planning of all aspects of the economy. Administering the system demands ingenuity because it is human nature to be individualistic and creative, but these characteristics tend to interfere with the operation of the socialistic state. Therefore, socialistic regimes attempt to control individuality and creativity, except at the top, by limiting the freedom of those at lower levels through rules and regulations and by the creation of bureaucracies.

> Any doctrine that . . . weakens personal responsibility for judgement and for action . . . helps create attitudes that welcome and support the totalitarian state.
> —JOHN DEWEY

Bureaucracy, whether socialistic or capitalistic, is established for one purpose: to create order. It is not equipped to accommodate individuality, freedom, or creativity, but it looks after order very well. So, as the bureaucracy grows, individual initiative is subdued.

> You have to have some order in a disordered world.
> —FRANK LLOYD WRIGHT

In the final analysis, the vitality of any organization depends on individual initiative, creativity, and entrepreneurial endeavor. But the socialistic-bureaucratic pyramid, with its stultifying regulations and red tape, dominates while the creative contributions of the individual deteriorate. When this happens, the socialistic society attempts ei-

ther to intensify the controls or increase individual
incentives. As in other societies, each solution tends to
cause the problem to proliferate, often in a circular
manner.

> Usually, terrible things that are done with the excuse
> that progress requires them are not really progress at
> all, but just terrible things. —RUSSELL BAKER

The Soviet Union has been in the business of centralized planning ever since the Revolution. It has produced
for itself nearly all our maladies, along with those peculiar
to its own system and ideology, including cycles of sur-
pluses and shortages, poverty, inflation, regimentation,
maldistribution, and political tyranny.

> Democracy is the art of running the circus from the
> monkey cage. —H. L. MENCKEN

Capitalistic societies, based on the concept of free enterprise and individual liberty, cannot exist for long in a
pure form because uncontrolled free enterprise leads to
monopolies that eliminate competition and ultimately cause
the destruction of free enterprise. Therefore, governments
subscribing to a democratic philosophy find themselves
making rules and regulations that limit free enterprise and
individualism, and creating bureaucracies to enforce the
rules and regulations. Governments committed to democratic principles are usually pledged to promote the common good or general welfare. If this is interpreted to mean
those good things that are common to all persons, then legislation regarding environmental protection, public safety,
and fair-trade practices becomes the legitimate domain of
such governments. Democratic countries, in attempting to
implement the concept of the common good, have estab-

lished bureaucracies to administer legislation concerning child labor, minimum wages, fair employment, union activities, health and safety, and monopolistic trade practices. What has evolved is still a basically capitalistic or free-enterprise system, but with checks and balances and growing bureaucratic controls that begin to rival those of the communist countries.

The Seal of Approval

At the age of eighteen, Russian-born comedian Yakov Smirnoff began to develop his act in his hometown of Odessa by entertaining his friends. Eventually, he applied to the government for a permit to be a comedian. His jokes had to be written and submitted to the ministry for approval. Smirnoff was accepted for the position and given a copy of the act he was permitted to perform. For the next ten years, he worked cruise ships in the Black Sea.

Five years ago, when he applied for emigration to the United States, his Soviet joke permit was revoked. He has resumed his career in America, where at least his jokes do not need the approval of the government bureaucracy.

What does he miss about Russia?

"I especially miss my favorite TV shows—The Young and the Arrested, One Day to Weep, Bowling for Food, Marx and Mindy."

The Peter Pyramid operates in both socialist and capitalist societies

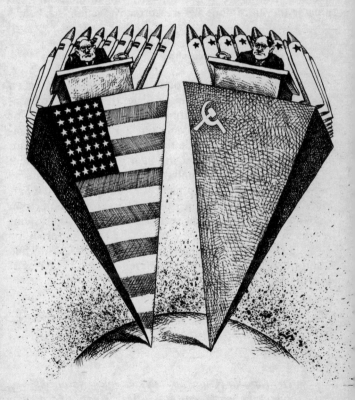

Of the world as it exists, one cannot be enough afraid.   —T. W. ADORNO

WHERE WILL IT END?

Once a bureaucratic procedure is instituted, it has great staying power. The larger the bureaucracy the more difficult it is to take corrective action. Furthermore, big bureaucracy is capable of big blunders, and the bigger the agency, the harder it is to rectify the mistake and the greater the harm done before corrective action is taken.

> Progress is a nice word. But change is its motivator and change has its enemies. —ROBERT F. KENNEDY

One agency is capable of creating confusion, but when more than one is involved in an issue, the capacity for confusion explodes. The Environmental Protection Agency for years has been trying to stamp out the use of certain cancer-causing pesticides, while the Department of Agriculture for years has been encouraging their use. The Department of Agriculture gives $65 million in subsidies to the tobacco industry, while the Department of Health and Human Services mounts a $5 million campaign to stop people from smoking. The convolution to today's bureaucratic systems results in the citizens of New York City being governed by 1,487 different governmental agencies and boards, while Californians pay a total of 454 different taxes on one loaf of bread.

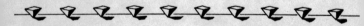

Full Circle

Dr. Lincoln Ralphs says that as a very young child he thought the world was flat. When he went to school he was told it was round. Later he was told it was spherical. In upper grades he was told it was an oblate spheroid. He got close to the truth at the university, where he learned it was a geoid. He looked this word up in his Greek dictionary and found that it means "earth shaped."

IS THE FABRIC UNRAVELING?

We are witnessing now the incapacity of nearly every government to support any longer the hopes, and in some cases even the lives, of its people. During recent times there has been a multiplicity of crises in every major institution, including law enforcement, education, the family, and the economy. All these trends collectively have been called the unraveling of the fabric of civilization. It is a picturesque analogy that has some validity, but many of the problems are the result of just the opposite of unraveling. They are not caused by the coming apart of the threads that hold the fabric together, but by the progressive weaving of millions of tangled threads into an ever more complex social tapestry.

The Plot Thickens

A notice was included along with utility bills in the San Francisco area: "One item of expense included in the rate increase recently granted to PG&E by the Public Utilities Commission, amounting to $177.4 million, was attributable to President Reagan's Economic Re-

covery Tax Act of 1981, which requires the Public Utilities Commission to charge rate payers for the expense of taxes which are not now being paid to the Federal Government and which may never be paid. This expense may increase in the future."

This entwining process, which has been going on gradually over the centuries, presently has accelerated to the stage where the pattern is so involved and each part so intricate that nobody can understand the whole picture, and only a few can understand any of its parts. The systems that have sustained us through the ages have become so complicated, administratively ritualistic, and densely intertwined that the inevitable outcome is stagnation and the near inability to cope with any problems at all.

> The tragedy of scientific man is that he has found no way to guide his discoveries to a constructive end. He has devised no weapon so terrible that he has not used it. He has guarded none so carefully that his enemies have not eventually obtained it and turned it against him. His security today and tomorrow seems to depend on building weapons which will destroy him tomorrow.
> —CHARLES A. LINDBERGH

WHO NEEDS INFLATION?

Over the past four decades the prices of food, clothing, shelter, and fuel have shot up along an unbroken incline, ending the economic stability and slow rate of inflation that had existed for generations.

This entwining process results in the near inability to cope with any problems at all.

> The cost of living has gone up another dollar a quart.
> —W. C. FIELDS

Most national governments are bankrupt and have been so for a long time. Bankruptcy is a condition wherein an individual or institution spends more than he, she, or it earns or takes in, and a point is eventually reached when debts cannot be paid in full. Usually nations do not renege on debts directly but do so indirectly by postponing payment and going deeper and deeper into debt or by printing more money of depreciated value. The national practice of paying off debts with such currency is similar to settling a bankruptcy at a percentage on the dollar value of the debt, except that government settles its debts at face value with deflated dollars and thereby continues to operate in a state of perpetual functional bankruptcy.

> Having a little inflation is like being a little pregnant—
> inflation feeds on itself and quickly passes the "little"
> mark.   —DIAN COHEN

Inflation is the printing of too much money and an overabundance of credit. The printing of too much money is the governmental response to the ever-present threat of terminal bankruptcy. Government blames its citizens for inflation and tells them to tighten their belts and to curb credit spending. But it is government that deflates the value of the dollar by printing money to keep its bankrupt economy afloat. It is the government of the country, not its citizens, that reduces the value of the currency. The only individuals outside of government who could effectively devalue the currency would be counterfeiters. It is government that must build its Peter Pyramid of inflation, layer upon layer, as an ongoing policy to cover up its unsound financial strategies. It is government alone that needs inflation.

Business as Usual

In March 1981, Poland, with a debt of $27 billion, said it simply could not raise the $2.5 billion owed to its creditors that year. In August 1982, Mexico could not pay the interest due on its debt of $80 billion. In January 1983, Brazil, with a debt of $87 billion, defaulted on a $446 million payment due on the principal. In fact, at the end of 1982, financially troubled developing and eastern bloc nations owed $706 billion to banks, governments, and international financial institutions. The International Monetary Fund reported that at the end of 1981, thirty-two countries were behind in their debt payments.

Today, all but one of the major U.S. banks has lost its triple-A credit rating because of loans extended to high-risk countries. If the borrowers default, the Federal Reserve will have to save the banking system, causing inflation to skyrocket. Americans would, in effect, share the cost of the banks' capricious lending policies. In addition to devaluation of the dollar, banks burdened with large defaults would have less money available for mortgage loans, car loans, and consumer credit.

If all the economists were laid end to end, they would not reach a conclusion. —GEORGE BERNARD SHAW

HOW BIG IS TOO BIG?

So far we have seen that the Peter Pyramid, the way systems have of starting out small and simple and growing large and complex, can have positive or negative results. It has positive results when the complexity allows us to achieve those things that would be impossible without a complex system. Obvious examples are the scientific research that has led to decoding genetic mysteries, modern electronic communications, and the space program. Negative results occur when large systems have been applied to rather simple problems. For example, the more complex the system of law becomes, the less law, order, and justice we have. We established government bureaucracy to avoid political patronage and we find we have a civil service that is seldom civil and rarely provides service.

Advice to Young Bureaucrats

Pressed for simultaneous noncoordinated decisions by pragmatic opportunists, it is best not to stampede into espousing contingency measures. Instead, peripherize your view of the motives and assess the repercussions through calling a meeting. Out of it will come the unpolarized, extramarginal consensus needed to make the decision comfortable. Failing this, allocate the effort among knowledgeable personnel thereby availing oneself of their expertise, and at the same time, optimizing distribution of responsibility, thus dulling the teeth of gnawing doubt.

—JOHN KIDNER,
from *The Kidner Report*

The size and complexity of a system must be appropriate to its function. A complicated system may be required for a complicated task, but any excessive complexity hinders accomplishment. Once an organization grows beyond human scale so that the individual becomes merely a functionary engaged in keeping the system going, the point of diminishing returns has been reached.

> Conformity, humility, acceptance—with these coins we are to pay our fares to paradise.
> —ROBERT LINDNER

Let us look briefly at public education as an example. In days gone by, public education was essentially a local matter, with the schools operated by elected school boards. Schools were run on the concept that formal education took place in classrooms and involved interaction between a teacher and a class of pupils. The school board's responsibility was to provide classrooms and teachers. The administration of the school was the responsibility of the head teacher or principal, who usually also taught the senior class. This system was simple, but it provided a satisfactory level of education to a large number of children. It was an uncomplicated system with a low level of bureaucracy and a high level of output. It is what might be termed a small system/large volume ratio.

Successful Small Systems

The plow is the most important agricultural implement since the dawn of history. In one continuous motion the plowshare cuts a furrow and the moldboard turns the earth to break up the soil, bury crop residue, and control weeds. In the mid-nineteenth century John Deere, an American mechanic, invented the highly efficient, one-piece, all-steel plowshare and moldboard that is favored internationally. This small and simple device produced a way of efficiently tilling vast areas of soil.

In modern times we have been witness to many similar examples. The silicon chip invented in 1970 leapfrogged over its electronic ancestors: the vacuum tube, the transistor, and the integrated circuit. This fingernail-size microprocessor effectively and economically did work that formerly required a number of cumbersome and energy-inefficient devices. These examples show that a small system can have a big output.

We have seen public education grow into a huge bureaucratic structure with agencies established at the federal, state, and local levels. Consolidation of small school districts into large school systems has replaced the little red schoolhouse with the large multipurpose school. The school is administered, at the district level, by a superintendent of education, who usually has a doctor's degree in administration, and by a staff of specialists. The school itself is run by a principal and a flock of assistant administrators, department heads, and counselors. Centralization of special services has made it possible for the district to have a curriculum director, a psychological services department, an instructional technology division, a staff of subject consultants and professional advisers, and a fleet of buses so that the large schools can serve the wider community.

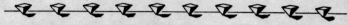

Education Informs and Enlightens

Recently a Houston, Texas, high school principal sent out an invitation to parents requesting their attendance at a meeting about a new educational program. The invitation included a description of the program which said, in part:

> Our school's Cross-Graded, Multi-Ethnic, Individualized Learning Program is designed to enhance the concept of an Open-Ended Learning Program with emphasis on a continuum of multi-ethnic academically enriched learning, using the identified intellectually gifted child as the agent or director of his own learning. Major emphasis is on cross-graded, multi-ethnic learning with the main objective being to learn respect for the uniqueness of a person.

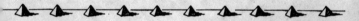

With all the federal, state, and local educational bureaucracy, and all the school administrators and consultants, it still appears that whatever education does take place happens in the classroom between a teacher and a group of students. But it seems that what happens between teachers and students is not much better than in earlier days. The addition of the monstrous educational bureaucracy has been accompanied by changes. More minority children are in school and pupils remain longer in the educational system, but the total amount of education may not have increased. It may just be spread thinner over an increased school population.

> It sometimes seems as though we were trying to combine the ideal of no schools at all with the democratic

1890

TEACHER   STUDENT   EDUCATION

1980

SUPERINTENDENT   INSTRUCTIONAL TECHNOLOGIST   DIETARY SUPERVISOR   CURRICULUM DIRECTOR

COUNSELOR   TEACHER   STUDENT   EDUCATION

> ideal of schools for everybody by having schools with-
> out education.   —ROBERT MAYNARD HUTCHINS

Today a public school education costs over $25,000 per pupil, and yet the graduate might not even be able to read. During the past twenty years the average verbal score on the National Scholastic Aptitude Test has dropped thirty-three points. Recently, in many parts of the country, the standardized Functional Literacy Test has been given. The test consists of basic reading and simple arithmetic, plus tasks such as filling out job applications and reading labels on canned goods. In one school district, 45 percent of the children failed the math portion of the test and 14 percent, the reading. This poor showing, in contrast to that of the schools of yesteryear, is an example of a large and complex system that is producing measurably poor results, another case of a high level of bureaucracy and a low level of output; constituting a large system/small volume ratio.

Educational Pyramiding Case Number 101

Every profession seems to include practitioners who delight in making the simple complex, like the teacher who told her fourth-grade class, "Here is the way to remember how to spell 'geography.' George eats old gray rats and paints houses yellow."

It is important when dealing with the concept of the appropriate size of a system that bulk or complexity not be

Goldberg's Bottle Opener

As you raise bottle (A) it pulls string (B) thereby jerking ladle (C) which throws cracker (D). Parrot (E) jumps for cracker. Perch (F) tilts upsetting seeds (G) into pail (H). Weight pulls cord (I) opening cigar lighter (J) setting off sky-rocket (K) which causes sickle (L) to cut string (M). Rock (N) falls flipping opener (O) opening beer bottle.

Combination Bottle and Can Opener

confused with volume. A system might handle a large volume of apples and still be comparatively simple—a small system/large volume ratio. Conversely, a complex system might handle only a small volume of apples—large system/small volume ratio. This distinction is essential to all discussions of the Peter Pyramid. Obviously, with the increase in population there is a need for more apples and education and all other products and services. But in talking about the growth of the Peter Pyramid, I do not mean the expansion required to accommodate an increased number of school children or a bigger crop of apples, but only the growth in size of the system through increased procedural complexities or bureaucratic expansion.

Ancient Chinese Insight

It appears that the Chinese had early insights into the nonthinking, nonresponsive bureaucratic processes that the Western world is just now beginning to understand.

In the sixth century B.C., Lao-tse, one of China's great philosophers, described how the bureaucrat could gain control of a country through purposelessness and inaction. In the Tao te Ching, *he states:*

> A state may be ruled by measures of correction; weapons of war may be used with crafty dexterity; but the kingdom is made one's own only by freedom from action and purpose.

In the eleventh century, Su Tung-p'o, a public official and a great poet, wrote:

On the Birth of His Son

> Families, when a child is born
> Want it to be intelligent.
> I, through intelligence,
> Having wrecked my whole life,
> Only hope the baby will prove
> Ignorant and stupid.
> Then he will crown a tranquil life
> By becoming a Cabinet Minister.

WHY RED TAPE?

Bureaucracy and red tape have become synonymous. The term "red tape" was derived from the red ribbon once used in England to tie folders of legal documents. English common law is based on precedent, so judicial decisions often demanded a search of the records. This required clerks and lawyers to spend a great deal of time untying and retying the red ribbons that bound the folders. It was only natural that those waiting for a decision or opinion, while the clerks carefully unknotted and reknotted the ribbons, made negative comments such as "More damned red tape," or "More red tape, more delay."

> Skewered through and through with office pens, and
> bound hand and foot with red tape.
> —CHARLES DICKENS

At first, red tape referred to just paperwork, but now it has become an offensive and disheartening symbol for a variety of meaningless or useless organizational practices, rules, regulations, procedures, and forms.

The more directives you issue to solve a problem the
worse it gets.   —JACK ROBERTSON

Today if you build a better mousetrap, the world will
not beat a path to your door, at least not until you comply
with government regulations having to do with labor rela-
tions, occupational safety and health, environmental impact, including air and water pollution, and product safety.
Your mousetrap advertisements will be within the jurisdiction of the Federal Trade Commission, and the U.S. Department of Justice is involved with your trademark,
copyright, and patents as well as your right to make a product that competes with those of established manufacturers.
Realizing that under these circumstances it is going to cost
a lot to get started, you decide to raise the money by the
sale of stock. You discover that you are now under the jurisdiction of the Securities and Exchange Commission.
Your study of potential markets shows that the mouse
problem is greater in foreign countries. In order to take
advantage of this large volume of business, you need an
export license from the U.S. Department of Commerce. In
acquiring employees you must comply with federal prohibi-
tion against sex, race, and age discrimination. You are required to file reports for social security, pension, tax, and
other purposes while complying with local licensing, building, and safety regulations. You must do all this while you
are trying to establish and run your business. You may end
up producing more government paperwork than mouse-
traps.

I am raising the question of whether people can understand and participate in their government when it
becomes so obscure and mired down in unintelligible
gibberish.   —JERRY BROWN

A Better Mousetrap

You might feel you are being required to comply with excessive quantities of meaningless red tape, or at least paperwork that does not apply to your mousetrap business. In your calmer moments, when you are more objective, you realize that you are in agreement with the purposes of many of these regulations. You do not want the community's water supply poisoned and you do not want the right to poison it, nor do you want anyone else to have that right. You feel the same way about the objectives of many of the other regulations, but you are still frustrated by all the red tape. It is the bureaucratic way of doing things that annoys you. Furthermore, every time they want information or money, they demand it immediately or they set a deadline and impose penalties. When you want something from them, they are nonresponsive or give you the bureaucratic runaround.

National Association of Professional Bureaucrats Speaks Up

On Tuesday, June 22, 1971, when Dr. James Boren, satirist and president of the National Association of Professional Bureaucrats, testified before the House Public Works Subcommittee on Investigation and Oversight, it was clear that a new leader had bubbled to the surface of the political cesspool. The subcommittee was conducting an inquiry investigating red tape, delays, and excessive paperwork. The committee had heard testimony that proliferating guidelines and review processes had added four and a half years to the time lag before an average stretch of highway could be built. It was also estimated that this growing delay fac-

tor added as much as $12 billion to completion of federal highway systems. The committee was told that some highway projects must be reviewed by as many as sixty-two different government agencies, and that one new requirement will add approximately eighteen million pages of paperwork annually to the existing load. A typical Corps of Engineers project consumes seventeen years from its congressional inception until the first spadeful of earth can be turned. Following this testimony, Dr. Boren, the bureaucrat's bureaucrat, was called upon to solemnly swear that the testimony he was to give would be the truth, the whole truth, and nothing but the truth. Boren's response was, in part, "All things are quite relative, you know, and to reduce so complex a matter to a simple categorical response of 'yes' or 'no' would seem under the circumstances to be thoroughly unprofessional. . . . It will be recalled from early times, those with responsibility for governmental affairs have been wary of the oversimplifications contained in such a question, as witness for example the response of the Roman procurator Pontius Pilate, who when confronted by a similar question responded with the well-reasoned reply 'What is truth?' If you will permit me to make one point perfectly clear, however, I should like to say that, within the context in which we normally define the relative abstraction of truth, it is expected that the underlying thrust of my testimony will serve the long-range ends foreseen by your question." He concluded his response by requesting permission because of a shortage of time to submit for the record a more complete statement setting forth his position on the subject of truth.

The following are a few statements made by Dr. Boren during his presentation as well as some of his answers to the committee members' questions.

"I come to these hearings, Mr. Chairman and

members of the committee, neither as an adversary to the fine work of this committee nor to the distinguished men who have given previous testimony. I do come to these hearings, however, with heaviness of heart because I have noted the sustained manner in which the committee has insisted in trying to reduce what it refers to as 'red tape' and to eliminate the lengthy delays involved in building highways, dams, and other public work projects.

"The committee's insistence on action may cause it to ignore the aesthetics of inaction.

"Number, quality, and time-related orbital referrals are basic keys to the postponement of decision interfacing, and I believe that this is reflected in the pattern of testimony already presented to this committee.

"Do we count the flakes of snow that give beauty and a sense of serenity to the countryside in winter?

"To deny a dedicated finger-tapper an adequate supply of paper on which to record the results of his prodigious pondering is to deny him the tools of creative nonresponsiveness.

"But all artists must have freedom to choose their own art form, some require massive canvases or reams of paper to express their message in great broad strokes, while some artists deal in miniatures and one-page memoranda that embody great detail and beautiful subliminal images.

"Instead, Mr. Chairman and members of the committee, I suggest that appropriate consideration be given to the quality of bureaucratic life and that more paper, not less, may be desired.

"Paper to the professional bureaucrat is as canvas to the artist.

"We have three guidelines in the National Associa-

tion of Professional Bureaucrats: (1) When in charge, ponder. (2) When in trouble, delegate. (3) When in doubt, mumble.

"This is the purpose of our organization. By steadfastly adhering to these principles and by fostering the utilization of constructive decision avoidance, we can reduce the rate of program and policy implementation and thus prevent mistakes from being made."

Historically, the responsibility for the construction of this vast network of red tape has been widely distributed. Nobody deliberately set about the creation of a red-tape jungle, but individual members of special-interest groups requested and demanded that certain policies, regulations, or constraints be imposed. These requests, when subjected to the political process and bureaucratic implementation, end up as a red-tape quagmire. Even groups with what appear to be broad public interests are each concerned with only a relatively narrow range of the total spectrum of government concerns. The Parent-Teacher Association, for example, has a different set of concerns about the future of America than do the Veterans of Foreign Wars. Conservation groups have a different interest in our natural resources than do petroleum, coal, and lumber companies. There are so many groups and so many diverse interests that there is little wonder we end up in a stifling tangle of red tape.

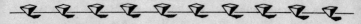

Do We Know What We Want?

We are a strange people. We spend our lives doing things we detest, to make money to buy things we don't need, to impress people we don't like. We never want to be doing what we're doing. When we eat, we read; when we watch TV, we eat; when we drive, we listen to music; when we listen to music, we work around the house. When we want to be with friends, we go to a noisy restaurant; when we want to party, we spend the evening trying to converse.

DEMOCRACY IN ACTION OR INACTION?

At this point it is appropriate to look at an example of how our democratic process works in building a bureaucracy.

> All life is a game of power. The object of the game is
> simple enough: to know what you want and get it.
> —MICHAEL KORDA

In times past, food and drugs were derived directly from natural sources. The consumer could evaluate the quality of most food products by their texture, aroma, and appearance. Once modern packaging and chemical food additives were introduced, the customer could be fooled by the picture on the box or by the chemically altered appearance, texture, aroma, and even flavor of the product. Today we have to read the fine print on the label to know what is in the product, so the government tries to protect us by passing honesty-in-labeling legislation. However, this is sometimes not enough. The consumer does not know which chemical additives are harmful or what quantity is dangerous until the government provides information from results of its testing.

> The food here is so tasteless you could eat a meal of it
> and belch and it wouldn't remind you of anything.
> —REDD FOXX

The government's first attempt to regulate the quality of drugs sold in America was the law passed in 1848 prohibiting the importation of adulterated drugs. It was not until 1902 that regulation of American pharmaceutical manufacturers was undertaken. Public outcry at the death of two children from tetanus-contaminated diphtheria antitoxin forced Congress to pass the Virus, Serum and Toxin Act.

> I learned why they're called wonder drugs—you won-
> der what they'll do to you.   —HARLAN MILLER

The Pure Food and Drug Act of 1906 became law because public concern was aroused by the exposure of unsanitary practices in the meat industry and by evidence that some meat was "4D"—it came from animals that were dead, dying, diseased, or decayed on arrival at the packing plant.

> All interest in disease and death is only another ex-
> pression of interest in life.   —THOMAS MANN

As new dangers were exposed, new rules were imposed. In 1937, more than a hundred people died from taking Elixir of Sulfanilamide containing highly toxic diethylene glycol. Congress enacted legislation in 1938 requiring new drugs to pass safety tests.

One of the new miracle drugs is inexpensive. That's
the miracle.   —HAROLD COFFIN

In 1958 a drug, thalidomide, developed in Germany
and hailed as the perfect sedative, was exported to several
countries. In 1961 it was withdrawn from the market because word leaked out that thousands of malformed babies
had been born to mothers who had taken thalidomide during their pregnancies. In America the drug was still on the
waiting list for Food and Drug Administration (FDA) approval. When it was revealed that under existing laws
thalidomide could have been approved by the FDA, Congress moved to have extensive, time-consuming, and expensive testing of drugs. Today the FDA is a huge
bureaucracy with such divisions as: (1) Bureau of Foods,
(2) Bureau of Product Safety, (3) Bureau of Drugs, (4) Bureau of Veterinary Medicine, (5) Bureau of Radiological
Health, (6) Bureau of Biologics, (7) Bureau of Medical Devices, (8) National Center for Toxicological Research and
(9) Regional Operations.

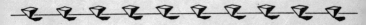

The Ultimate Protection

*In Satellite Beach, Florida, a health department of-
ficial closed down a sidewalk lemonade stand operated
by an eleven-year-old boy. The reason given was that
the proprietor had failed to provide rest-room facilities.
The health department official explained, "We're just
trying to protect the health of the public. We're not
picking on little boys."*

Nowadays, with the availability of so many highly potent but extremely toxic drugs, and with the widespread use of chemical food additives, the FDA provides a much-needed service in testing substances and in publicizing results. Before the FDA's existence, however, the consumer's only protection was through the courts. The purchaser of contaminated or poisonous food or drug items could sue the producer or merchant. This redress of grievance, or after-the-fact approach, was unsatisfactory in cases where prevention was the objective or where fatalities occurred.

> I'm not afraid to die. I just don't want to be there
> when it happens.   —Woody Allen

If public-safeguard agencies were eliminated, we would be worse off than we are now. More people would die or be harmed by contaminated food, adulterated milk, or falsely labeled items. More investors would become victims of financial manipulators and unscrupulous stock speculators. Damage to the environment would escalate, without government safeguards.

> The people's safety is the highest law.
>   —Roman legal and political maxim

If we accept that certain government services are essential and only direct our efforts to elimination of nonessential agencies, we are often surprised to find how many defenders the "unnecessary bureaucracy" has. This is an outcome of the nature of government in a democratic society. In its attempt to accommodate and regulate the widely varying ánd sometimes diametrically opposed interests of its citizens, it enacts complicated and conflicting legislation. It is still difficult for the citizens of a nation born out of a revulsion of overbearing government to accept that they are helpless in the face of their own oppressive bureaucracies.

Change of Address

When an Illinois welfare recipient dies, the state welfare department automatically sends him a note informing him his benefits are being discontinued because of his death. No records are available indicating how many dead welfare recipients have received their notices.

If we don't like the way government does things, do we have an alternative? Who is better able to do the job of taking care of the needs of this nation? You? Me? Chrysler? Lockheed? The New York Central Railroad?

> The legitimate object of government is to do for a community of people whatever they need to have done, but cannot do at all in their separate and individual capacities. —ABRAHAM LINCOLN

We should oppose, with every means at our disposal, the encroachment of bureaucracy and the meaningless complication of our lives by government agencies or by commercial interests and private organizations. In doing so, we should be aware that this is only a partial solution or preventive measure. Many of the systems of government, industry, and society are necessary. The solution to the problems created by the overwhelming Peter Pyramids of our modern world is to redesign the systems so that they better serve human needs for security and fulfillment.

> If we do not learn from history, we shall be compelled to relive it. True. But if we do not change the future, we shall be compelled to endure it. And that could be worse.   —ALVIN TOFFLER

5

Pyramid Proficiency

The more complex the system becomes the more open it is to
total breakdown.   —LEWIS MUMFORD

In this final chapter we will look at some of the processes
that can offer us a measure of protection from the Peter
Pyramid Syndrome. We cannot just dismantle the base-up
pyramids that are presently threatening life, liberty, and
the pursuit of happiness and return to a simpler past. Progress has provided too many benefits that would be lost.

The people who are always hankering loudest for
some golden yesteryear usually drive new cars.
                              —RUSSELL BAKER

The proposed solutions are not intended as cure-alls to
be applied randomly to any or every problem without first
conducting a careful diagnosis. It is diagnosis that provides
the initial key to cure.

The danger of the past was that men became slaves.
The danger of the future is that men may become
robots.   —ERICH FROMM

When a business enterprise is having difficulty because of excessive bureaucratization of its administrative processes, an accumulation of deadwood in its executive suite, red-tape strangulation, or any of the other symptoms of the Peter Pyramid Syndrome, diagnosis will reveal where changes should be made. When a government agency is top-heavy with accumulated fat, or plagued with bureaucratic tumors that impair its function, it may need surgical treatment. When surgery is called for, however, it requires the skillful wielding of a scalpel, not hewing with an ax.

> The best way to escape from a problem is to solve it.
> —BRENDAN FRANCIS

Of all the resources we have at our command that could lead to solutions for the pyramidal problems we have created, it is only our capacity for creative thought that holds promise. It is only our minds with their unique processes that are the true problem solvers.

> The long path from material through function to creative work has only one goal—to create order out of the desperate confusion of our time.
> —MIES VAN DER ROHE

The world is full of problems; the solutions require ingenuity, innovation, or creativity. When it is determined that a real problem exists and when a solution is desired, we engage the services of creative individuals with the required expertise. Once the problem is resolved, or becomes easier to handle, the creative individuals are replaced with less creative persons. The creator is needed to establish solutions; the conformist is needed to institutionalize the solution and keep it going.

Autocracy is one-man rule, bureaucracy is rule by rules. The one aims at making things happen, the other at making things orderly.
—Eugene E. Jennings

If we are going to have a viable and efficient society, there is a need for both the creator and conformist in every organization. The creator is the innovator, the change agent, the problem solver. The conformist is the bureaucrat, the supervisor, the clerk devoted to control and to the achievement of known, predictable, measurable goals or products.

The art of progress is to preserve order amid change and to preserve change amid order.
—Alfred North Whitehead

The solution to systems or organizational problems would appear to be simple—maintain enough conformists in each organization to keep order and accomplish the routine tasks along with the creators, in order to make changes and improvements to keep things from bogging down and becoming an unresponsive bureaucracy. A few of the more progressive bureaucrats exercise minor ingenuity but apply it only to small-scale improvements of existing methods. The bureaucratic structure can accommodate changes, such as mechanization, of some repetitive and predictable functions.

Creative activity could be described as a type of learning process where teacher and pupil are located in the same individual.
—Arthur Koestler

The effect of the bureaucracy on the creator is either to force him out of the organization by requiring him to

submit to boring, routine work or to stifle his creativity and
let him lapse into bureaucratic apathy.

> In a study of the management of conflict within groups
> . . . that contained a "deviant"—a person who ag-
> gressively sought solutions to problems and forced the
> group to confront conflicting views and integrate
> them—came out with richer analysis of the problem
> and a better solution. When, as the next step, each
> group was asked to throw out one member, the
> "deviant" was thrown out every time! —DAVID J. SICA

The creative individuals, upon whom real change or
improvement of the system depend, are outnumbered and
overwhelmed by the control-minded conformists intent on
formalization, standardization, and unchanging ritualiza-
tion. The conformist may be a busy person with a complex
job to do. He must handle quantities of paper and decide
the channels for various documents. Likewise, pieces of paper are channeled to his desk. When a document arrives at
his department, and there is no routine for handling it, he
calls for suggestions or it is referred for study. He proposes
little. He listens, consults, reads reports, and makes assign-
ments. He collects reports and distributes the jobs-to-be-
done. We value ability but usually settle for stability.

> The real problem is what to do with problem solvers
> after the problem is solved.   —GAY TALESE

The creative person questions routines, attacks the existing way of doing things, and speculates about things
never done before. The conformist resents the disrupting
influence of the creator, and the creator resents the frustra-
tion of not being allowed to try new ideas. Because of the
overpowering influence of bureaucratic conformism, special

The effect of the bureaucracy on the creator is either to force him out of the organization by requiring him to submit to boring routine work or to stifle his creativity and let him lapse into bureaucratic apathy.

effort is required to keep the creative individual within the system.

> It is the function of creative men to perceive the relations between thoughts, or things, or forms of expression that may seem utterly different, and to be able to combine them into some new forms—the power to connect the seemingly unconnected.
> —WILLIAM PLOMER

The following six recommendations suggest areas that need the unique problem-solving abilities of creative individuals. The first five recommendations are not presented as solutions for all problems created by the specter of the base-up pyramid. In some cases they may be applied as preventive measures and in others as remedies for specific ailments.

> The anguish of our times is the Frankenstein monster that has been created by our convenient and long silences. We reap this anguish because we have encouraged its growth by pulling the bedclothes over our heads, hoping that the ogres might go away and that dawn might purify all. —JOHN B. KEANE

The first five also directly concern government bureaucracies. The remedies range from termination of agencies to corrective modification of programs. Corrective action is frequently preferable to the economic chaos and social havoc caused by massive, across-the-board cutbacks in programs.

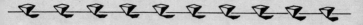

Efficiency Guidelines

1. Do not waste time reading irrelevant information.
2. If notice does not apply, destroy before reading.
3. If contents of envelope are inappropriate, return without opening.

The sixth recommendation, Pyramid Simplification, is broadly applicable to business and government and can be of benefit to organizations of any size. Simplification results in improved effectiveness, productivity, and service at a reduced cost. This is more consistent with the concept of a cure than the first five recommendations. Pyramid Simplification is not only a cure for the Peter Pyramid Syndrome, but it provides a means by which we can move forward from our present accomplishments to a better world.

> The more one knows, the more one simplifies.
> —ELBERT HUBBARD

Let us consider the first five prevention patterns.

1. FOREWARNED IS FOREARMED

Awareness of the Peter Pyramid and how it affects organizations or systems can be a preventive measure in itself. Many billion-dollar programs undertaken by governments might never have gotten beyond the initial planning stage had sufficient thought been given to how big, complicated, costly, ineffective, and counterproductive they could become.

For example, the Aswan Dam was built, at great expense, to produce electricity that was intended to be used to raise the living standard of the Egyptian peasants. Unfortunately, the dam generated an undesirable side effect. It withheld the Nile floodwaters so that the rich fertilizing sediment was deposited in Lake Nasser instead of on the land farmed by the peasants. The fields must now be artificially fertilized. Huge factories have been built to produce the chemical fertilizers. These factories use enormous amounts of electrical power and the dam's generators must operate at full capacity just to meet the fertilizer needs created by building the dam.

> China has four times the population of the U.S. within a land area of roughly the same size. With intensive labor, scrupulous conservation of resources and recycling of human and animal wastes, the Chinese are feeding and supporting themselves without outside aid. —DONALD MACINNIS

Many government projects and corporate programs have been started with the best of intentions, and have grown into pyramidal pork barrels or bureaucratic monsters that are difficult to feed, maintain, or get rid of. Good intentions are not enough. We must learn which questions to ask, and then we must answer them.

Pyramid Becomes Prison

The American philosopher, William James, observed that lives based on having *are less free than lives*

Year by year we are becoming better equipped to accomplish the things we are striving for. But what are we actually striving for? —BERTRAND DE JOUVENEL

based either on *doing* or *being. Our lifestyle is a proof
of that statement. We are surrounded by labor-saving
devices and yet have little real leisure. We have an
abundance of choices, but even at the supermarket,
where 53,000 new flavors, brands, sizes, and varieties
of products have appeared in the last ten years, much of
what we buy does not improve our standard of living or
serve any real purpose. In accumulating possessions,
we build our own base-up pyramid, and as it expands it
imprisons us.*

In our quest for having, we give up our freedom.
                                        —WILLIAM JAMES

*My daughter had a doll named Ann that she took
with her everywhere. As she played with the doll, she
fantasized that Ann could do all the things a real baby
could do.*

*My granddaughter has just received a doll capable
of developing diaper rash. She already has a number of
specialized dolls. One came equipped with prepared
dolly food, a spoon, and a package of diapers. Another
has her own tub, soap, and towel. Others include a sick
doll with her own thermometer, stethoscope, and medical kit; a fashion doll with several wigs, a comb, a
brush, a hair dryer, and six complete outfits of clothing;
a walking doll, a talking doll, and a teen doll that develops breasts when its arm is raised.*

*My daughter used her imagination to know when
her dolly cried, ate, drank, was ill, or slept. It gave her
a sense of security to have an imaginary friend and
someone to take care of. It seems likely that my granddaughter will continually expand her collection of spe-
cialist dolls, but they will never satisfy her emotional*

*needs because it is difficult to have a satisfactory rela-
tionship with a committee of specialists.*

2. THE INCREDIBLE HULK

Some events are too incredible to anticipate. If the
Founding Fathers had foreseen that democracy would be
perverted into a network of pyramidal bureaucracies not
accountable to the people, they probably would have established rules by which overcostly, ineffective, or offensive
agencies and programs could be dissolved.

Go West

*You might not know that 86 percent of the land in
Nevada is owned by the federal government, but it is
common knowledge to many farmers, ranchers, land
developers, and politicians in that state who try to exercise some local control. Under the guise of the Forest
Service, the Bureau of Land Management, the National
Park Service, the U.S. Department of Defense, and a
host of other agencies, the feds also hold deeds to 64
percent of Utah, 64 percent of Idaho, 52 percent of
Oregon, and 45 percent of California. East of the
Rockies only 1 or 2 percent of the land is under federal
control. It appears that eastern bureaucrats are not hesi-
tant to annex land in the West.*

The mortar that holds together the Peter Pyramid of the government bureaucracies is money. Curtail funds and the unwanted pyramid will self-destruct.

> Money is the symbol of duty, it is the sacrament of having done for mankind that which mankind wanted.
> —SAMUEL BUTLER

3. MOLEHILL OUT OF A MOUNTAIN

Every time government does something for the individual that he could do for himself, it impairs that individual's self-sufficiency. Every act of bureaucratic authority that diminishes citizen self-reliance in turn increases the demand for more regulations. To reverse this process, government should do only those things the citizen or taxpayer cannot do for himself. And as citizens we must be willing to shoulder those responsibilities.

China Policy

The Chinese appear to understand bureaucracy better than any other people in the world. They believe that bureaucrats should leave their offices and live with the citizens they are supposed to serve.

If our federal education officials had to spend one month each year in a ghetto school; if our Bureau of Mines officials had to spend one month a year in the dust, damp, and dark of a coal mine; or if all bureaucrats had to live with problems they were supposed

to solve or with the people they were supposed to serve,
they might be more responsive to our real needs.

Federal government should only concern itself with doing those things that state government cannot do. Likewise, state government should do only those things that city and county government cannot do. This would drastically reduce the federal bureaucracy and pare down the top-heavy pyramids at all levels so they become more stable structures.

> The consolidation of power in the political capital was accompanied by a loss of power and initiative in the smaller centers; national prestige meant the death of local municipal freedom.   —LEWIS MUMFORD

Although excessive centralization of authority results in bloated federal bureaucracies that are out of touch with local problems, it is important that the solution be a genuine move to restore local autonomy and not just an excuse to cut budgets and get rid of responsibilities by dumping them onto the next level down.

Studies of American and Japanese business management have shown important differences of style. These differences explain why American employees' productivity lags behind that of the Japanese. One of the unique features of Japanese management that contribute to employee loyalty and output is the way workers are treated when the company experiences financial difficulty. The Japanese start by cutting back at the upper levels of the organization and work down. First, they cut corporate dividends. Next, they reduce salaries and bonuses of top management. This is followed by trimming salaries of middle management. The last measure is to request the rank-and-file to accept pay cuts and reductions in the work force through attrition. Before terminating employees, management tries to find work for them in a subsidiary division. American organizations respond to economic difficulties by starting layoffs at the bottom and working up, usually never reaching the top. The Japanese method is a means of reducing the top-heavy structure of the Peter Pyramid.

> Our institutions are failing because they are disobeying laws of effective organization which their administrators do not know about, to which indeed their cultural mind is closed, because they contend that there exists and can exist, no science competent to discover those laws.   —STAFFORD BEER

4. AT THIS POINT IN TIME

If we were to establish fewer permanent agencies and appoint more ad hoc citizen task forces, we could avoid continuing our current pace of bureaucratic escalation. A one-time task force assigned to resolve a specific problem by a specific date is less likely to acquire self-interest fat, and even it if does, the task force is dissolved when its time is up and its findings are published.

Small Is Beautiful

"The cultivation and expansion of needs is the antithesis of wisdom. It is also the antithesis of freedom and peace," wrote Ernst Friedrich Schumacher in his

Our best protection against bigger government in Washington is better government in the states.
—DWIGHT EISENHOWER

eloquent book Small Is Beautiful, *subtitled* Economics
as if People Mattered. *A society that rejoices in the fact
that it continually converts luxuries into necessities is
bound to become victim of the Peter Pyramid. As
Schumacher points out, "We are suffering from a meta-
physical disease, and the cure must therefore be meta-
physical," and he concludes, "What is at stake is not
economics, but culture; not the standard of living, but
the quality of life."*

*As individuals, we are free to shift our concern
from the standard of living to the quality of life. We can
apply Schumacher's concepts so as to avoid complicat-
ing our lives unnecessarily, thereby realizing a higher
human potential.*

For further reading, see Small Is Beautiful *by
Ernst Friedrich Schumacher (Perennial Library,
Harper and Row, 1975).*

5. A WORD TO THE WISE

Much of what goes on today at even the highest levels
of government lacks what used to be called wisdom.
Wisdom or common sense is human mental activity lying
somewhere between the processes of pure logic and intu-
itive thought. There was a time when common sense based
on wisdom was a highly prized virtue and those who had it
were held in great esteem. Benjamin Franklin became an
American hero through *Poor Richard's Almanac*, containing his witty and wise aphorisms. Over the years Americans developed this popular utilitarian philosophy into
common sense, which means drawing shrewd conclusions
from accurate observations.

> Nineteenth Century scientists actually classified man as Homo Sapiens—man the wise. How foolish of them. Man the clever, if you like; man the brainy, man the intellectual, but not man the wise. Wisdom is very different from cleverness.   —STANLEY SYKES

In this century we have apparently underestimated the need for wisdom. With computers, satellite communication networks, and electronic calculators, what need have we for old-fashioned horse sense? Look around and the answer is obvious.

> More than any other time in history, mankind faces a crossroads. One path leads to despair and utter hopelessness. The other, to total extinction. Let us pray we have the wisdom to choose correctly.
>   —WOODY ALLEN

Computers are spectacularly competent in the area of machine logic, numbers, or mathematical computations, but are helpless when it comes to value judgments and everything else that can't be added up. We know how to do almost anything, but we often don't know how to assess the value of what we do. Without the uniquely human capacity for wisdom and good value judgment, we do things to our detriment, but still take pride in our efficiency in accomplishing them.

Voluntary Simplicity

The object of voluntary simplicity is a lifestyle that is outwardly simple and inwardly rich. Research indicates there is a growing trend in America toward living simply, avoiding excessive consumerism, and thereby achieving a better balance between the material and nonmaterial components of life.

Each individual who voluntarily decides to limit the growth of his base-up pyramid of possessions reduces his demands on the entire social system and thereby contributes to its simplification.

By resisting the temptation to complicate your life with unnecessary possessions and financial indebtedness, you can break out of the vicious consumer circle that so many are caught up in. Among those who have joined the Voluntary Simplicity movement are some of the most creative and capable intellectuals, artists, and humanistic capitalists in the country.

Voluntary Simplicity is a way to take control of your life. It is a way of clearing away what is not of value to you and replacing it with what is of true value. You can keep trying for more money, more possessions, and more status, or you can reorganize your life so that you do more of what you really want to do. If you decide to shift from a preoccupation with your standard of living to more concern for quality of life, start by asking:

1. Does what I buy basically satisfy needs or do I buy much that complicates my life or serves no real need?
2. Does what I buy complicate my lifestyle by requiring installment payments, maintenance, and repairs?

Those who have deliberately set out to simplify their material and financial existence have found that they have more time to devote to enriching the intellec-tual, spiritual, emotional, and aesthetic aspects of their lives. They have more energy to invest in love, fun, ex-ploration, healthful recreation, and the peaceful enjoy-ment of nature. Through a better balance between inner and outer values they have achieved a satisfying equi-librium between physical and material well-being along with an improved psychological and spiritual life.

For further reading, see Voluntary Simplicity *by Duane Elgin (William Morrow, 1981).*

Much of what needs to be done to remedy the prob-lems of our Peter Pyramids involves the use of common sense. It is through common sense that we can learn which questions to ask, find how to prevent new bureaucratic Pe-ter Pyramids, determine which funds to curtail, decide on the allocation of social responsibilities, and assign the pri-orities, funds, and personnel.

> Common sense in an uncommon degree is what the world calls wisdom. —SAMUEL TAYLOR COLERIDGE

6. PYRAMID SIMPLIFICATION

The Peter Pyramid Syndrome is the result of the accu-mulation of unnecessary complications in the systems we use to conduct our industrial, corporate, and governmental lives. Simplification of these systems eliminates only the un-necessary elements. It would not be a sign of wisdom to bring in a giant demolition machine with a wrecking ball

Voluntary Complexity

and start knocking down pyramids indiscriminately. Although the bureaucratic Peter Pyramids have earned our resentment or even outright hostility, such violent retaliation could be counterproductive. We would be in danger of losing too much of value along with the undesirable elements. What is required is more the touch of a sculpting knife, trimming away the excess to reveal the essence around which each pyramid was originally begun. Each organization then becomes a more trim, upright pyramid with a more stable structure.

> Man may even manage to defuse the time bomb around his neck, once he has understood the mechanisms which make it tick.
>
> —ARTHUR KOESTLER

TECHNOLOGICAL AND PRODUCT SIMPLIFICATION

The history of mankind has been a constant climb up the ladder of technological success. Much of this progress has been the result of reduction of complexity. We identify a problem and then look for a solution. Pneumatic tires were developed because tires of solid rubber failed to absorb enough of the vibration experienced in the early automobiles. This was a complex solution, involving tires and tubes made of natural rubber. Every car carried a set of tire irons, a jack, a pump, and a tire repair kit. Vast plantations were required to supply the natural rubber and fiber used in tire construction. Eventually the introduction of synthetic rubber, and the development of the tubeless tire, resulted in a stronger, longer-lasting, and more deflation-proof product that took less labor and material to manufacture and maintain. The tubeless radial tire is an example of achieving more with less—the essence of pyramid or system simplification.

> Many dramatic breakthroughs in science, engineering, and administration have been based on a concept of simplicity. This involves the discovery of a principle which enables a simple idea or simple machine to supercede a more complex idea or machine.
> —ARTHUR B. TOAN

The ballpoint pen is another example. It is not simpler than the nib pen, but if we consider the whole process of writing and the need for a highly portable writing tool that produces clear, readable ink copy, the ballpoint pen is a great simplifier. It not only eliminates the need for inkwells, but makes writing simpler in many other ways. It is no longer necessary to have a bottle of ink, a blotter, and a pen wiper. Now you can write, uninterrupted by having continually to dip the nib in ink or to fill the bladder of your fountain pen. No longer need you blot freshly written copy. Just as the nib pen was easier to use than the old-fashioned quill pen, the ballpoint pen further simplified writing through the elimination of time-consuming nonessentials. It achieves more with less. Simplification of a process is not always simple.

> The world has moved from the wire to the wireless, the track to the trackless, the visible to the invisible. More and more can be done with less and less.
> —R. BUCKMINSTER FULLER

Before the development of the Xerox dry-copy process of reproduction, making photocopies was a multistep procedure using a negative and a wet chemical process. The Xerox process eliminated the negative copy and the extra steps, saving both material and labor. Again, more has been achieved with less.

> The one best way is always the simplest way—once it is learned. —FRANK BUNKER GILBRETH

The traditional light switch made its electrical connections through solid metal contacts that were subject to wear and malfunction. The invention of the mercury switch solved this problem. Elimination of wear through use of mercury gave us switches that will last almost indefinitely.

> The one consistently natural thing is to try by intelligence and imagination to improve on nature. —BRIGID BROPHY

Modern jet engines eliminated the need for propellers while increasing load capacity and speed; oral polio vaccine eliminated the often painful use of hypodermic needles; drip-dry clothing eliminated the need for ironing; and pantyhose eliminated the necessity for garters.

> Creativity is merely a plus name for regular activity . . . any activity becomes creative when the doer cares about doing it right, or better. —JOHN UPDIKE

In each of these technological achievements, we have received more for less. Metaphorically, each is an instance of small system/high volume ratio.

> We must recognize the power and value of technical simplicity as distinguished from the complexity that we too often regard as sophistication. We have tended to ignore something that the best Paris dress designers, and Sir Isaac Newton, never forget: the ultimate sophistication is simplicity itself. —THOMAS V. JONES

TOTAL SYSTEM PERSPECTIVE

Although the introduction of new technology into an outdated or overly complex system often results in simplification, in some cases just the opposite occurs. New technology can increase the complexity of a system without improving its overall effectiveness. Whether a new component will simplify or complicate a process can be determined only by viewing the entire system. We must be able to see the whole process, its objectives, each of its parts, and how they all interact, or we might end up with an undesirable outcome: large system/low volume ratio.

> Complication is often the path of least resistance for the designer. It is either the result of lack of knowledge or lack of adequate thought. The simple way of doing something is not usually the one that first springs to mind.   —ARTHUR E. RAYMOND

In the days of sailing ships, freight was placed on horse-drawn wagons and hauled to the dock. It was loaded into the ship's hold by human muscle power. At the end of the voyage, the process was reversed as the ship was unloaded and the cargo delivered. This pyramid of labor-intensive stevedoring went on for hundreds of years.

> In every age "the good old days" were a myth. No one ever thought they were good at the time. For every age has consisted of crises that seemed intolerable to the people who lived through them.
> —BROOKS ATKINSON

As trains, trucks, and steamships with power winches were added to the stevedoring pyramid, it became more and more technically complex. Cargo was hand-loaded on trucks and hauled to warehouses where it was unloaded and stored. Later it was taken out and reloaded in boxcars and transported to loading docks. Here it waited in storage sheds until the ship was ready and its place in the hold was available. Then it was moved manually up the gangplank by longshoremen with handcars, or by steam-powered derricks, to be packed by hand in the ship's hold. At the port of destination, unloading involved as many steps as loading. In the overall system, each cargo item was handled many times, by many people.

> I have met a few people in my time who were enthusiastic about hard work. And it was just my luck that all of them happened to be men I was working for at the time.   —BILL GOLD

The invention of the standardized cargo container made it possible to pack the goods only once, move the whole container by flatbed truck or train to the freighter, and unpack it only once at its point of destination. Through the introduction of a standardized container to the freighting system, cargo now receives better protection in transit. Breakage, pilferage, and damage from exposure to wind, rain, and seawater are reduced. Labor, loading times, and cargo losses are only a fraction of previous levels.

> The important thing is not to stop questioning.
> —ALBERT EINSTEIN

The container itself looked like a minor innovation, being merely a boxcar or a truck body without wheels, but the entire concept created a cargo-handling revolution. The new standard container replaced a series of costly components in the cargo-handling pyramid, such as the truck body, the boxcar, the warehouse, and the storage shed at the dock. It also increased the deck-load capacity of the traditional freighter and made possible the development of today's highly efficient container ships. One standard component replaced four major and many minor components, and it does the job cheaper, faster, easier, and better.

ADMINISTRATIVE SIMPLIFICATION

The same concepts used in these examples of product and process simplification are applicable to business and government. The overall objective of administrative pyramid simplification is to do more with less,—that is, reduce red tape, streamline procedures, eliminate malfunctions and delays, and do the total job cheaper, faster, easier, and better—to create a small system/high volume ratio.

> One has to look out for engineers—they begin with
> sewing machines and end up with the atomic bomb.
> —MARCEL PAGNOL

To understand such simplification we must view the pyramid as a system. But effectiveness in management is more difficult and trickier by far than technological simplification where the physical parts, the process, and the product are evident.

A simplified machine is one that has no unnecessary parts. We can see that most tires no longer have tubes and that jet planes have no propellers, but it is much more difficult to know whether an administrative procedure, law, or regulation is essential to the management of a company or to a state or federal government program.

> And there is no greatness where there is not sim-
> plicity, goodness, and truth.   —LEO TOLSTOI

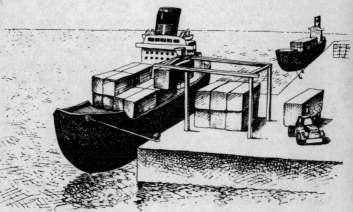

Any third rate engineer or researcher can increase complexity; but it takes a certain flair of real insight to make things simple again.
—ERNST FRIEDRICH SCHUMACHER

One goal of improving a machine or a work process is to achieve increased output. To evaluate the quality of administration or management in the same way might encourage the building of the bureaucratic Peter Pyramid. Increased work output, more statistics, more paperwork, and more cases being processed may be irrelevant to overall program effectiveness. Writing more reports that do not get read or are not understood is counterproductive. Collecting excessive or unneeded data decreases office profits and effectiveness. Releasing unprocessed statistical data in meaningless profusion creates confusion and misunderstanding.

> The very technology that makes our living simple, makes society more complex. The more efficient we get, the more specialized we become and the more dependent.					—THOMAS GRIFFITH

A major problem in management is that competence in an executive or a bureau chief is primarily an abstract idea. An executive or a chief administrator should be paid to think, to decide, and to manage. He should deal primarily with intangibles, such as concepts, assumptions, and values.

> Out of intense complexities intense simplicities emerge.					—WINSTON CHURCHILL

Bureaucrats, executives, and managers tend to occupy themselves with activities that keep them from the thinking and conceptualizing required to achieve maximum simplification and operational effectiveness of their businesses or programs. Many spend their time buried under mountains of paperwork, attending meetings, arranging conferences, endlessly returning phone calls, and waiting for late reports. Only a small fraction of the bureaucrat's or business manager's time is spent on actual innovative, system-level thought-work.

> The man who has begun to live more seriously within begins to live more simply without.
> —ERNEST HEMINGWAY

Today's management gap is being filled by a stream of exotic electronic and computer-based office machines, microcomputers, and multi-terminal word and data processors. These processors can receive, send, or generate information by a telephone voice command. They are linked to a master-computer memory bank that automatically produces, stores, and retrieves reports and research. Efficient as these electronic marvels are, and as great their promise, the potential Peter Pyramid hazards are equally great. An office or agency equipped with a computer, word processors, a Xerox duplicator, and an electronic mailing system has an unlimited capacity to escalate its output of useless reports, meaningless statistics, or pointless memos. In the hands of a corporate or governmental bureaucrat, unmotivated by the concept of pyramidal simplicity, the computer can become a monster with an uncontrollable appetite for data. The data system becomes the means of trying to satisfy the monster, and you are the source of those data.

> Anyone brave enough to challenge the idea that in a few years the replacement of man's brains will be the top industry of the nation is in danger of having his brains amongst the first to be replaced.
> —SIMON RAMO

In the industrial age a wrench in the works could stop the machine. In the computer age it could stop the world.

SMALL BEGINNINGS

There is no question that modern technology has greatly improved some pyramidal systems in ways that affect our everyday lives. Libraries in some communities now keep their book catalogs on microfilm and microfiche rather than on file cards. In some libraries you can even ascertain via microfiche whether the book you need is anywhere in the entire library system, and at what library, so that it can be ordered for you. Less time spent and more service.

> Our life is frittered away by detail . . . Simplify, simplify.
> —HENRY DAVID THOREAU

The computer has made it possible, in some states, for drivers with good safety records to renew their licenses by mail, rather than by standing in line at the department of motor vehicles. Less time, more service.

> Anything one man can imagine, other men can make real.
> —JULES VERNE

Because of the computer, voters in some states can register or change their voting address by mail, rather than seeking out a deputy registrar at a supermarket. Again, less time and more service.

> The computer is not intelligent at all but very stupid indeed, and that, in fact, is one of its great values—its blind stupidity.
> —SIDNEY LAMB

In Fresno, California, many city-planning operations have been automated. A computer using up-to-date information about population densities, vacant property, and other relevant data is able to provide decisions about building permits more quickly, more objectively, and more efficiently than are employees poring over information stored in files. City planning has a more comprehensive and current information base, and the information is integrated in a manner and at a speed beyond the capacity of the human brain. Advanced technology simplifies the planning process for the employees and does a better and more consistent job—achieving more useful decisions with less bureaucracy.

> From naive simplicity we arrive at more profound simplicity.   —ALBERT SCHWEITZER

A bird's-eye view of traffic flow along a city street shows that vehicles move in surges caused by traffic signals. Much of the time, the vehicles are not moving but waiting for a green light or for the right-of-way. The time when vehicles are stopped in traffic lanes while waiting for a signal, plus the time lost in accelerating and decelerating, along with the delays caused by stalled vehicles, constitute the time the roadway is not in full operation for its intended purpose of moving traffic. If traffic could be managed so that it could flow instead of stopping and starting, a street could accommodate many more vehicles without increasing the number of lanes and thereby achieve more with less.

> Rush Hour: That hour when the traffic is almost at a standstill.   —J. B. MORTON

In Baltimore this has been accomplished with a system that eliminates unnecessary stops. When a vehicle passes over a wire-loop sensor embedded in the roadway, it induces an electromagnetic current that is conducted over the regular telephone wires to a central computer. The computer receives the message that a vehicle is approaching an intersection. The computer controls the traffic signals according to the needs of the vehicles in the street. The red and green traffic lights operate on a variable time schedule controlled by the amount of traffic in the respective lanes. Right-and left-turn signals are operated in relation to the traffic in the turn lanes. This arrangement maximizes the traffic-carrying capacity of the street, simplifies the task of driving, saves fuel, reduces accidents, decreases driving time, and lowers the demand for traffic officers. More traffic is accommodated more efficiently and safely by increasing the capacity but not the size of the streets—more with less.

> This new development, automation, has unbounded
> possibilities for good and for evil.
> —NORBERT WIENER

With these examples of the successful application of systems analysis to civic problems to inspire us, let us take the next step and apply system simplification to bureaucratic-administrative problems.

> Order and simplification are the first steps toward the
> mastery of a subject.   —THOMAS MANN

DIGITAL AND ANALOG THINKING

The computer and its many satellite electronic devices for office automation have the potential for becoming effective components in a simplified management system, but only if top executives are aware of the danger of too much reliance on computer readouts as opposed to value judgments. This situation can be viewed at two levels, the digital and analog.

> Computing machines perhaps can do the work of a
> dozen ordinary men, but there is no machine that can
> do the work of one extraordinary man.
> —E. B. WHITE

It is at the digital level that the computer and the other electronic machines can make their greatest contribution to system simplification. A computer can process vast amounts of data quickly, and present them in a comprehensible form so that a better-informed decision can be made. The potential of office automation is fulfilled when its administrative productivity in one department is integrated so as to contribute to the effectiveness of the total system, and is compatible with the procedures and equipment in all other departments within the system. The best equipment poorly utilized or wrongly applied could be like using the space shuttle for delivering interoffice memos.

> In character, in manner, in style, in all things, the su-
> preme excellence is simplicity.
> —HENRY WADSWORTH LONGFELLOW

As an aid to the kind of decisions I have to make throughout the day, I prefer an analog watch to a digital watch. The analog watch has an hour hand and a minute hand that point to the time; the digital watch gives a direct numerical readout. A glance at my analog watch and I know that the time is 9:48. The position of the hands also tells me I have 12 minutes to make my 10 o'clock appointment, and I am also aware from the hands' position that it is 33 minutes since 9:15 when I left home. Initially, learning to read and understand an analog watch is more complex than directly reading the numerical display of the digital watch, but the analog watch gives me much more than the time of day.

> Americans have more timesaving devices and less time than any other people in the world.
> —DUNCAN CALDWELL

The digital watch gives me only one piece of information, the numerical time. If I want to determine how much time I have left before my appointment or how long I have been traveling, I have to do some mental calculations. My analog watch gives me all this information visually, which helps me make appropriate value judgments and decisions about my behavior in the next 12 minutes.

> Wisdom denotes the pursuing of the best ends by the best means.
> —FRANCIS HUTCHESON

Analog thinking involves a total system perspective, which goes far beyond the limits of digital thinking. I am driving my car in the middle lane of three lanes of southbound traffic at 55 miles per hour. This digital information tells me that I am traveling at a reasonably safe, legal speed. The truck ahead of me slows down. I have three choices other than running into the back of the truck. I can apply the brakes and slow down. Or I can try to pass the truck in either the right or the left lane. My perception of traffic in these lanes, including the speed of oncoming traffic, gaps in the traffic, and road conditions, will influence my decision. Each of these three choices is based on an analog decision or value judgment, and not one is made by glancing at the speedometer.

ANALOG CLOCK

Digital Watch

> Men must be decided on what they will not do, and
> then they are able to act with vigor in what they ought
> to do.   —MENCIUS

It is at the analog or value-judgment level that the interaction of all the components of the network (human, electronic, mechanical, and procedural) must be related if we are to achieve effective total system management. An effective system of interdependent elements is more than the sum of its parts. It is as unlikely that we could achieve collective unity in a piecemeal way as it would be for the proverbial team of chimpanzees, randomly hitting the keys of ten thousand typewriters, to write *Hamlet*. Management improvement is best achieved from the top down. Holding our leaders accountable for simplification in and improvements of their pyramids is one of the best executive motivators. Without total system perspective and commitment to pyramid simplification, we can end up with procedural improvements that have little significance to ultimate overall performance—like rearranging the deck chairs on the *Titanic*.

> It is better to be ten percent effective in achieving a
> worthwhile goal than one hundred percent efficient in
> doing something worthless.   —SID TAYLOR

In the simplification approach to halting and reversing the mindless escalation of the Peter Pyramid, analog thinking provides the values, purposes, priorities, goals, ideas, principles, possibilities, and risks, as well as the concept of pyramid simplicity. Digital thinking utilizes data, numbers, averages, ratios, formulas, probabilities, and other statistics.

> If you put tomfoolery into a computer, nothing comes
> out but tomfoolery. But this tomfoolery, having

> passed through a very expensive machine, is somehow
> ennobled and no one dares criticize it.
> —PIERRE GALLOIS

Both analog and digital thinking are required to ensure balanced judgments in the decision-making process. Using the full capacity of our decision-making abilities, human and electronic, in the resolution of total system problems will clarify, simplify, and expand our effectiveness.

> Unless there be correct thought, there cannot be any
> action, and when there is correct thought, right action
> will follow.   —HENRY GEORGE

SIMPLIFY FOR SUCCESS

In modern times no government has discovered yet how to simplify the Peter Pyramids of Bureaucracy. Few have even tried, though examples of beginnings in this direction are available. As in the case of technological and product simplification, once the process of pyramid simplification is under way, more effective and efficient methods will be discovered.

> I am for a government that is vigorously frugal and
> simple.   —THOMAS JEFFERSON

With the evidence of bureaucratic proliferation all around us, with the warnings of the Peter Pyramid to motivate us, and the solutions of pyramid simplification before us, let us be the first to adopt a high resolve to move forward to a system that is more economical, easier to operate, less prone to defects, and more effective.

Simplify for Success

ABOUT THE AUTHOR

DR. LAURENCE J. PETER was born to poor but pompous parents in his native province of British Columbia, Canada, where he received an extensive but inadequate education. He now realizes how well off he was before he began facing reality and feels he owes much of his success to a solid sense of his own inadequacy. Although he doesn't have many faults, he takes full advantage of the few he has. If he had his life to live over again he would make the same mistakes earlier.

His books have achieved great popularity in spite of his unswerving integrity. He makes us see the funny side of things that aren't funny. Dr. Peter claims he never thinks when he writes because it is impossible to do two things at the same time and do them well.